The *Real* Is Unknowable
The *Knowable* Is Unreal

Other Works By Robert Powell

Beyond Religion

The Blissful Life

Christian Zen

Crisis in Consciousness

Dialogues on Reality

Discovering the Realm Beyond Appearance

The Free Mind

J. Krishnamurti: the Man and His Teachings

Path without Form

Return to Meaningfulness

Why Does God Allow Suffering?

Zen and Reality

Edited Works

The Essence of Sri Nisargadatta Maharaj

The Experience of Nothingness by Sri Nisargadatta Maharaj

The Nectar of Immortality by Sri Nisargadatta Maharaj

Talks with Sri Ramana Maharshi (First American Edition)

Towards the Openness by Douwe Tiemersma
(Translated from the Dutch by Frank Anderson)

The Ultimate Medicine by Sri Nisargadatta Maharaj

The Real Is Unknowable
The Knowable Is Unreal

From the Notebooks of
Robert Powell

North Atlantic Books
Berkeley, California

Published by: North Atlantic Books
Berkeley, California 94712

Cover and book design by Jan Camp
Printed in the United States of America
Distributed to the book trade by Publishers Group West

The Real Is Unknowable, The Knowable Is Unreal is sponsored by the Society for the Study of Native Arts and Sciences, a nonprofit educational corporation whose goals are to develop an educational and crosscultural perspective linking various scientific, social, and artistic fields; to nurture a holistic view of arts, sciences, humanities, and healing; and to publish and distribute literature on the relationship of mind, body, and nature.

North Atlantic Books' publications are available through most bookstores. For further information, call 800-337-2665 or visit our website at www.northatlanticbooks.com. Substantial discounts on bulk quantities are available to corporations, professional associations, and other organizations. For details and discount information, contact our special sales department.

Library of Congress Cataloging-in-Publication Data

Powell, Robert, 1918–
The real is unknowable, the knowable is unreal / by Robert Powell.
p. cm.
ISBN 1-55643-553-3 (pbk.)
1. Advaita. 2. Philosophy, Hindu. I. Title.
B132.A3P66 2005
181'.482—dc22
2005003885

1 2 3 4 5 6 7 8 9 DATA 09 08 07 06 05

Acknowledgments

Portions of this book have been reproduced in *The Mountain Path* Journal, Tiruvannamalai, India.

I would like to express my special thanks to Yvonne E. Cárdenas for the expert manner in which she has edited this work.

Table of Contents

Prologue

$\mathcal{H}$istorically, most approaches towards a better understanding of man and his universe have been pursued within more or less well defined scholastic areas, with as yet little liaison or contact between them. In more recent times, with the advent of the specialist, this trend has become even more pronounced. Science, philosophy, medicine, and psychology carry on merrily in their respective courses, without much regard for any unity underlying all knowledge. Thus, each develops within a watertight compartment, with its own language or jargon that is often not even understood by any of the other disciplines, and each having its own methodology for probing the unknown.

It seems to me that specialization in any field inevitably introduces limitation and distortion of one's vision, not only because specialists usually end up "knowing almost everything about almost nothing," as the saying goes, and therefore what they know is hardly worth knowing, but also because in the very process of specialization something in

specialist – expert →
curiosity thwarted –

the overall picture gets lost that is very essential to man's understanding; each of the existing approaches being inherently fragmentary, the end result must necessarily be of a like nature. In other words, the integration of a great deal of fragmentary information can never lead to a reliable or accurate picture of the Whole; or, as it has been summarized: the Whole is more than the sum total of its parts!

Is a reverse approach possible, one that starts with an examination of man's entire existence and then fills out the picture by studying the various details? Recently, with the realization of the close interrelationship of body and mind, there has been a certain rapprochement between medicine and psychology leading to the new branch of psychosomatic medicine; but this is a relatively rare example of what can be achieved through the building of bridges between various disciplines. And even here we are some way yet from the total acceptance of non-duality that does not recognize any absolute divisions between mind and matter, between the material world and the biological world, between one individual and another.

To this writer, a different approach exists towards knowledge and insight. It is not a novel approach, having been known in some areas of the world for thousands of years, but is presently largely anathema to orthodox learning. It takes as its point of departure the entire field of experiential existence, the whole of consciousness. In this attack on the unknown, one ruthlessly refuses to be sidetracked by detail, assumption, speculation, or knowledge—and, inherently, all knowledge is partial or fragmentary. One comes to an integral understanding by close examination, coupled with extensive explorative contemplation, of a very few pertinent facts. Because the investigation is in-depth, penetrating to the very foundation of our knowing and thinking, and thereby contacting the non-dualistic substratum of all manifestation, it does not become yet another form of specialization. Such exploration must necessarily lead to realization of the Emptiness that underlies all existence, which as the source of everything unites the various disparate aspects of our existence. This will not only put an end to all doubts, but open up an entirely unexpected vista of tremendous magnitude and beauty, making our vision truly whole. In the ensuing pages we will attempt to view any subject primarily in relation to that Wholeness, so that we may acquire the deepest possible insight into the life of man. Once having seen the great truth of non-duality or *advaita*, we can then return to the various individual branches of learning with greatly enhanced understanding. We will be able to work within the artificial barriers separating the various disciplines without being hampered by them in any way. One might call this "working within the system yet not being of it."

Part One: Reflections

$\mathcal{W}$isdom is to reject conventional wisdom about almost everything.

❈ ❈ ❈

$\mathcal{L}$ike the man who does not realize how dangerous driving actually is, and thus is a danger to himself and others, so a man who does not understand thinking really is a dangerous person. Because thinking lies away from reality and is always a projection from the unreal, it is no more than a dream. The non-stirring of the dream is peace and bliss.

❈ ❈ ❈

$\mathcal{T}$ime is an invention, a creation of the mind. During dreamless sleep, time does not exist. Thus, one may wake from deep sleep lasting only a couple of hours and feel one has slept the entire night. In dreams, there is time because the mind is active, but it is different from that experienced during the waking state. Even in the waking state, during pure perception without mentation of any kind, a state exists without time.

Likewise, during deep sleep, space does not exist. But in the waking and dream states, space is created by the activities of the sense organs and the brain.

⁂

*D*oes the body actually exist? We perceive the body with the senses, but the senses are part of the body themselves. What this amounts to is that the body says that the body exists. Its testimony is immediately suspect, tantamount to taking at face value the statement of the thief that he is honest.

⁂

*U*ltimately, we can say only that there are sensate impressions (being perceived by the senses). But what is the meaning of that? How can this statement be further reduced in terms of ultimate reality? It cannot. All statements about reality are void. This is the beginning of seeing into Emptiness, the beginning of true wisdom.

⁂

*I*n true *advaita*, or non-duality, there is no denial of the existence of good and evil. These are considered inherently and necessarily co-existent with the Universe, the mind, space-time. As is stated so succinctly in the *Ashtavakra Gita*, "The Universe is merely a mode of the mind; in reality it has no existence." Just as in a dream we are emoted by all kinds of things which upon awakening are seen to be products of a restless mind, so upon awakening to our real condition, we understand that our waking state experiences are equally the products of a dream factory and that in the Absolute none of these things exists. Thus, the only way of coming to terms with "evil," and participating in the Bliss that is our birthright is by transcending the limitations of body, mind, and world.

✤ ✤ ✤

*R*eality can never give rise to unreality, since what flows from existence will inevitably be in the realm of existence. But the alternative does not add up either, for what is illusory or non-existent cannot give rise to Existence or to anything for that matter: A fruitful example of the use of Reason in *Vichara* (spiritual inquiry)!

✤ ✤ ✤

*B*ody perception gives rise to a framework in space and time that drives and motivates all our thoughts and actions. This total mechanism is nothing but what we call "mind"— basically a concept, kept alive artificially through repeated false vision and self-misunderstanding.

To pierce our suffocating illusion, we should see "body" as nothing but an easy way of speaking, a thought construct. We perceive "body" as such because we assign limits or boundaries to it in space and time. These boundaries have been assigned by the sense organs, which are themselves part of the body whose real existence has yet to be proved. So the whole thing is an exercise in begging the question—a circular argument!

✢ ✢ ✢

All that we really are is an "idea," everything that we think to have "existence"—i.e., independent existence—is only a concept, a creation of the mind.

✢ ✢ ✢

Most of us like to have some "temporary immortality" to temporarily negate our ideation or "ideological" reality. We constantly negate the fact that our being is a mere idea. Because once I accept or confirm my existence as mere idea, where am I? Nowhere at all. I am a nothingness, however, that rests on the solid basis of consciousness.

✢ ✢ ✢

*O*nce I have understood conclusively that the self is no longer that exclusive structure of flesh and bone that I had habitually called "I" or "me," then I am free from any idea of differentiation in and of reality. I look into this boundless Emptiness, which is at once the Plenitude. This is *advaita*— the insight into the true nature of what *is*.

❀ ❀ ❀

*W*hen you use that word "I," what's the first thing you think of? The "body." Do not say "your" body, because that is the fundamental first mistake from which all others follow.

Fundamentally, our thinking revolves around that "I" imagination or projection. Where is thought, without the latter?

Without the "body," which "I" have projected, where is the world, and where is the mind?

Truly, there is only Consciousness!

❀ ❀ ❀

*E*verything is but Imagination, and that is the only Truth . . . fully grasping this signifies the end of logic.

❀ ❀ ❀

The truth about the meaning of life is that there is none, just as the mind that would postulate it, as well as space and time, are all non-existent.

⁂ ⁂ ⁂

Death can exist only in the world of form. And form itself is non-existent; it is a kind of waste product of the brain/nervous system, which itself is also part of the exudate.

⁂ ⁂ ⁂

Tragically, we have built the whole of Existence upon our perception of the entity designated as "I" or "self."

The idea of "body" comes about through integrated sense data, which in turn are physical reactions to stimuli. The latter only register because of the underlying substratum called "mind." In its absence, they would not be able to manifest, just as in the sleep state there is no registration of anything happening around us.

⁂ ⁂ ⁂

People are concerned with the injustice of "when bad things happen to good people." But what about "when good things happen to bad people"? The former affirms our usual dualistic mode of functioning (good always gets rewarded or should be). Questioning this world outlook could be the starting point of a non-dualistic or *advaitic* realization.

❈ ❈ ❈

*W*hat is man, if he is not that "I-am-ness" bundle of concepts and images, which has come upon him at birth? Either he is the Consciousness or Absolute, or he is the total negation of Reality. There is no reason that the state after death should not be identical to the state before birth. If man were essentially *nihil,* totally non-existent, then the manifest state of body-mind could not have arisen. Therefore, what one is, the Self, is the eternal Consciousness, the Unmanifest, which brings forth the "I-am-ness," space-time, and the entire world or worlds.

❈ ❈ ❈

*T*he state beyond sleeping and waking, beyond life and death, is "Consciousness."

The state beyond "you" and "me" is not "It." Termed "Consciousness," Nisargadatta Maharaj also uses the word "beingness," but stresses this is still a precursor to the Ultimate state.

❈ ❈ ❈

The majority of people in this world confess to a belief in the existence of a God of some kind. But is this any wonder, considering that they themselves have created this concept in the first place, and then have added this term to their vocabulary?

⚜ ⚜ ⚜

Once again it must be stated that it is so much easier to repeat and accept something one has heard than to question everything regardless of its source. Our propensity in this direction is constantly exploited in the areas of religion and politics.

⚜ ⚜ ⚜

Truth depends on a frame of reference, reality does not.

⚜ ⚜ ⚜

The senses advise us of the presence of a (or "the") world. But the senses themselves are part of this world, so such advice is useless, as we are merely engaged in a circular argument.

⚜ ⚜ ⚜

What is the Self and what is Consciousness? There is a special difficulty analyzing these particular terms and fully comprehending them in meaning and ultimate validity. This is simply due to the fact that every term in our language represents a concept or abstraction. The Self or Consciousness forms the sole exception. The truth of the matter is that even the word "comprehending" does not apply here, since it is entirely a question of realizing—that is, sharing its reality, becoming one with it, not having a conceptual relationship with it. We are dealing with the fact that every subject can be seen as comprising a subject and an object, since the subject itself can be viewed further as an object to a second observer-subject.

✣ ✣ ✣

People who look superficially at the teaching of Nisargadatta Maharaj may observe that it is apparently very close to that of the materialists who posit that matter produces consciousness just as the liver produces bile. But it is equally true that the body is the product of consciousness, it being a mental reflection, an apparition that comes and goes in consciousness and can therefore be nothing but consciousness. Without consciousness, where is the body? Without Consciousness, as in deep sleep, where is the world, where is anything at all? It is much like a chicken-and-egg type of proposition.

✣ ✣ ✣

Both the body and the mind have a deeper foundation, a substratum, from which both arise and into which both return, in an ever-recurring cycle. That substratum is the Absolute, which itself is not affected by time.

✤ ✤ ✤

Man is everlastingly talking about reaching out to the Supreme, but has forgotten that he himself has projected this Godhead or Supreme in the first place. Through thinking, observing, and meditating, we hope to acquire knowledge of our fundamental nature, thereby forgetting the basic parameters of our being, through which we aim to acquire this transcendental knowledge. All knowledge gathered in these efforts is ultimately based on sensory perception.

✤ ✤ ✤

The bodily senses are said to constitute a window on the world. The question, however, is whether the senses (i.e., the body) are separate from the world. In order to provide valid knowledge, the instrument for knowing has to be separate from that which it wishes to know, to understand. And not only separate but also greater and more fundamental in scope. Only in the latter case will the knowledge acquired have any relevance, any meaning. The ocean can know an ocean droplet, but the latter will never have an inkling of the nature of the ocean.

Since the senses are no other than the body, we are actually talking about a cyclic process: the soma pronouncing on the soma, and even expressing itself in terms of the soma—clearly a circular process and paradox. The organs of perception and any conceptions based on their findings are completely useless in grasping the fundamental nature of oneSelf! These findings will ever be fragmentary and incapable of knowing the Whole, one's real identity, the Self.

⁂

*T*he cultivation of the life of desire and satisfaction drains our vital energy and keeps us bound to the false image of the body. In itself satisfaction is not wrong, but exclusively living for satisfying desires, whether bodily or mentally, keeps us in bondage and strengthens the illusion that we are this bundle of thoughts and concepts. Since the ego is a process that consumes nervous energy in order to set itself apart from the rest of the universe, every time we engage in the desire-satisfaction game we drain away valuable energy and postpone the moment of our eventual emancipation. Unlike other members of the animal kingdom, we have a superior brain stem, which has actually put us at a disadvantage in this respect.

⁂

*I*f indeed the world has come about as if by magic, how can anyone take that world seriously? And how can anyone rationally cling to that apparition?

Our functioning in the world is as a body-mind entity, and takes place within innumerable frames of reference, each of which contains relationships that are valid within a particular frame of reference. These frames of reference are our worldly relationships, relationships of relative truths. Individually, these frames of reference have significance with respect to each other, but collectively their value is void, not being grounded anywhere. They are like clouds in the sky or images in a dream.

✤ ✤ ✤

*T*he Indian teacher Sri Atmananda once stated that the existence of dreams is a real blessing because it grants us the possibility of contemplating the waking life as nothing but a dream. If the waking state were all we ever knew, then the idea of our existence being a mere dream could never have arisen. The waking state would have solidified our prevalent dualistic worldview.

✤ ✤ ✤

*I*s it not amazing, this cycle of knowing and unknowing, and their ultimate unification? One begins by not-knowing anything—*avidya*—participating in the cycle of *samskara,* under the light of Ignorance, with the idea that there is something to know. One is compelled to proceed in this way, and eventually ends up at one's starting point, namely that one does not know, but this time with a slight, or perhaps huge, difference—depending on one's point of view: the realization that there is neither knowledge nor anything to know. Thus, one starts off being an ordinary agnostic, and ends up as a very special type of agnostic—one who does not know but also, and more importantly, one who knows very clearly that there is absolutely nothing to know because even the idea of there being any one thing is erroneous.

⁜ ⁜ ⁜

Science is reputed to give us facts only, nothing as speculative as conjectures. But in actual fact what it gives us only are correlations, where the correlates are further conjectures.

⁜ ⁜ ⁜

To see the usefulness of everything is knowledge. To see the uselessness of everything is wisdom.

⁜ ⁜ ⁜

Brahman, i.e. the Absolute, Consciousness, or the Self—whatever one wishes to call it—is to be known only through non-dualistic ways of knowing—which is actually "knowledge transcended." Can one still speak of "knowing" in this connection? And *Maya* can never be "explained," mainly because that which is giving the explanation is in itself *Maya!* When the proverbial "flatlander" tries to explain his world, it is always in terms of his unrecognized handicap, his restricted two-dimensional perspective, and therefore sadly unaware of the real three-dimensional world around him!

⁂ ⁂ ⁂

Brahman is uncreate, for the simple reason that creation could only be a projection by the mind, and would necessitate a preceding state of absolute Nothingness. Such an absolute state of Nothingness would be logically irreconcilable with the notion of "creation," for by definition no "event" could take place in it. Also, a created Brahman would imply a beginning point and therefore its involvement with space-time, which is *Maya.* That would mean that Brahman would be dependent on *Maya* for its being, when in fact the exact opposite is true. Brahman as the sole unchanging reality, could not be Brahman, by definition, if it rested upon space-time.

⁂ ⁂ ⁂

Even on the semantic level alone, the term "agnostic" has a certain significance. For when we use this term, we imply the opposite of our natural default condition. Semantically, there is no appropriate term for the latter's condition, for "Gnostic" has a very specific, sectarian meaning that has no relevance in this context. We postulate that "knowing" is our natural way of being, with its tremendous tableau of imagery. Immediately a certain value judgment is implied, which fundamentally shapes our entire being! We have loaded up on an enormous amount of mental baggage that henceforth conditions and oppresses us as inherently free human beings.

The moral is: Neither an agnostic nor its opposite be! Be your full capacity, be the Self only!

⁂ ⁂ ⁂

*T*he popular saying is "Seeing is believing." For me, seeing is neither believing nor disbelieving, neither accepting nor rejecting, but an immediate knowing that needs no corroboration.

⁂ ⁂ ⁂

*W*ho is that "me"? It is nothing but a false continuity—a memory of identification with the bodily senses, stretched out in time.

⁂ ⁂ ⁂

Can we realize or imagine a Reality in which there is the absence of Self or of Consciousness?

To understand anything, one should be able to look at it dispassionately or objectively. Here, there is no question of doing that. Since we are the Self, the Consciousness ItSelf, what is there with which to look at It objectively? Could there be anything with which to look at the Consciousness? No, of course not. There is only That, which we are ourselves, the ultimate Subject.

❊ ❊ ❊

All thought is essentially Imagination and therefore dangerous to one's spiritual health.

❊ ❊ ❊

Although we have the impression that we are born into a universe of time and space, the reality is actually the opposite: we ourselves project both time and space; that is, we "individualize" ourselves. The "individual" is in her true state only when dreamlessly asleep. On waking up (physiologically, that is) a certain "stirring" takes place, setting off a dream in which one imagines there are "others" who are contemporaries, who have lived before, and who will live after us. One further elaborates upon this condition with various theories of reincarnation and biological and spiritual evolution, all based upon an erroneous concept of time. One is totally unaware that within a "person's" life, all "others" are included, and the latter exist—that is, they are born and die—only to the extent that they represent their own consciousness.

❉ ❉ ❉

*I*nterestingly, "history," in its entirety, is always now; History is ever My-story. Another way to see this is that he and I are not actually separate; they both are only the Self or Consciousness. In non-duality, the physical act of perception remains the same as in duality, but its meaning is fundamentally altered.

❉ ❉ ❉

*T*rue spirituality is knowing the difference between things happening to "me," with their attendant pain and pleasure, and things just happening, with their attendant bliss.

❉ ❉ ❉

*W*e have taken so many things for granted in the spiritual life and the search for our real identity. In the first place, I have a serious doubt about the validity of using the mind in the search for self-realization. In this endeavor, are we not limited by the mind's circumference—that is, its innate limitations? It is important to realize that the only instrument available for investigation is the mind. But, unfortunately, its energy is wasted on the creation of an infinite web of thought.

Much spiritual effort has been misdirected toward the pruning of thought, the cultivation of goodness, and more generally the substitution of one set of desires for another. The teachings of Ramana Maharshi point the attention directly to the "thinker," to the originator of this world of thought. Self-enquiry, with its focus on the individual or the subject, takes one away from looking without—away from the realm of thought, from the ever-moving waves to the ever-still vastness of the ocean. The effort we speak of here is to hold on to the "I am," the core of one's being. Effort as a continual redirection of the attention is needed so long as we do not have a firm hold on the "I am." This is quite different from what we usually understand by the term "effort," which is the direction of thought in a particular direction. The question then arises: how do we know whether our attention is firm, or the mind is slipping back into its old thought patterns? If thought subsides while we are fully awake, we have held the attention on "I." When thoughts re-emerge, it means that our attention has strayed and the mind has returned to its usual pattern of activity.

# # #

*I*t is a curious situation that the two parameters upon which we most depend in determining our identity—the body and the mind—are treacherously unreliable and deceptive. Each cannot stand alone without the other, so neither can exist as independently real: The body depends for its definition and determination upon the mind, and the mind in turn depends for its definition and expression on the body!

The two pillars upon which we had depended for understanding and expression of our identity appear to be nonexistent. We are forced to conclude that our identity lies mysteriously far away from body-mind and is therefore simply ineligible for expression as such. The most important conclusion that we can draw from this situation is that what we are is irreducible to being an entity of any kind, and that this—the Infinite—can never be defined as mere concept or in terms of the known. Such is the inscrutable nature of our Self.

# # #

*S*pirituality is nothing other than clearing all cobwebs from one's mind, and the final realization that the mind itself is nothing but a cobweb too, obscuring the Self.

⁂

*T*o discover the reality of Self, it is crucial to discover that the composite of body and mind (and/or consciousness) is not just floating in an ocean of nothingness, the Void. If the latter were the case, one would verily and solely be that body-mind entity, and there would be some justification for the ruling materialistic outlook of society.

The non-local and non-locatable nature of body-mind implies that body-mind per se has no independent existence from the Void. I cannot define the entity without invoking the nature of the Void, since I am the Void, the Totality, the Self. Body or mind cannot be defined in terms of itself; it needs the mind or consciousness to do so. And consciousness is obviously in itself non-local and non-locatable; it is only matter that can be thusly defined. Hence, what we are in essence is beyond any form of identification or definition. This entire insight is represented by that code word, the "Self."

⁂

*P*erhaps our greatest danger, our greatest hindrance, in understanding ourSelves in what is real, is to stipulate that non-existence is real. In fact, true non-existence does not exist; it is a mere facet of our imagination. The antithesis, existence versus non-existence (life versus death), is a projection by the mind. Self exists unqualifiedly—beyond space and time. Generally, we do not "get" this because we live by, in, and for, the mind.

✤ ✤ ✤

*U*ntil there is not the slightest contact left with the world of thought and materiality, not even the tiniest speck, there will be fear of death. The realization must dawn that what we are in essence is spaceless and timeless, not to be confined within any form or tangibility. When the illusory appearance disappears, we manifest as the unchangeable purity of the Self.

✤ ✤ ✤

*A*t some point in one's inquiry one will inevitably arrive at the mind-blowing insight that the consciousness that explores the nature of the Totality or Consciousness is itself also that Consciousness! Full realization of this fact—even for one thousandth of a second—gives one sufficient pause to call off the search: "Thou Art That."

✤ ✤ ✤

*A*wareness is our ultimate nature, our very being. Actually, there is nothing else. Is there ever a moment when one is not aware? Awareness underlies our various levels of attention; it is ever there even when we are not paying the slightest bit of attention. Awareness is absolute, it has no degrees to it; attention flickers and wavers. Awareness is not relative: if you think it flickers like a flame, then it is not awareness; it is part of one's thought process or imagination.

✤ ✤ ✤

*T*here is the idea that something always has to be managed—a relationship, whether with persons or with "things"—and I am charged with the handling thereof. This idea I have imposed on myself is incorrect. One is already in the present moment, and this is always so.

✤ ✤ ✤

*W*e might think there are objects disturbing our awareness, but this is not so. Our awareness is steady; what changes are the objects only. Objects are relative; awareness is absolute.

✤ ✤ ✤

*W*hen I identify myself with any objects of awareness, through the play of the imagination, I misidentify myself; I make myself finite and insignificant in the light of awareness, which is infinite.

⁜ ⁜ ⁜

*T*urn your attention to what never moves, what is always there regardless of circumstances. The idea of "me" comes and goes—by identifying with it, you forget your real identity, which is always present. If your being were contingent on your presence in moments of calm, it would be a pretty limited "you" would it not? Real equanimity or contentment does not lie this way.

⁜ ⁜ ⁜

*I*n true meditation, we discover how we are the slaves of thought and so always live in the past, and consequently project a false future. It is important to be in the present, to realize we are the present and that it is all that ever exists, regardless of any disturbing thought. Realize that one is not the body, which is a basic error in one's outlook. Root it out, or rather leave it alone. End the mistake of maintaining the "I-am-the-body" idea, which is the root of all evil, and it will leave you, naturally, without need for repression. The false cannot survive in the light of truth!

Part Two: Interchanges

VISITOR: The other day we were talking about the screen of consciousness upon which the images of perception are projected. This analogy has been used for a long time, its origin probably being the cave wall and images cast by the light of the fire. Yet an analogy is helpful only insofar as it is apt at all points. I have been thinking about this aptness or lack thereof, and would like to communicate these thoughts.

If images appear as consciousness, they are apparition only, having no more tangible, independent existence than a dream. All world experiences then are dreamlike, including the experience of body and mind. In short, everything is consciousness, period.

If images appear in consciousness, like a fish in water, then there are two: the images and the consciousness. As a fish can be removed from the water and is different than water, so the images can be separated from consciousness and are different from consciousness.

If we think of images as being projected onto a screen that develops them, or actualizes them, or realizes them as a model for how being occurs, then we are left with a false duality. We create names, such as "projected images" and "screen of consciousness," yet until these so-called projected images interact with that screen, they have no existence whatsoever. Yes, we have named them "projected images," and given them a separate reality in word only; but in fact, they do not exist. We can name the cuts on a diamond "facets" and think of them as independent, but the facets cannot be removed from the diamond. Images are not separate from consciousness; facets are not separate from the diamond.

Consider manifestation as the multifarious expressions of the face of God or the Absolute. This eternal face has an infinite variety of expressions, which constitute life. Can one then say that the changing expressions come and go, are transitory in nature, and therefore are not the real? Can one say that the face behind these expressions is changeless and therefore is the source, the real?

Again, a face cannot be separated from its expression. The expression on the face is the face, and the face is the expression; there is no separation. And the images of consciousness are just as real (or unreal) as the consciousness. If, then, consciousness or awareness is the source, then so is the expression of that consciousness. The experiences and perceptions, which constitute life, far from being illusion, are the real. What else can they be but the Absolute, the unconditioned?

ROBERT POWELL: Your argument would indeed hold water if the real and the unreal would constitute one seamless continuum. But they don't! By no stretch of the imagination can the Absolute be understood or visualized in the ordinary way. The ordinary way—that is, the mind way—is ever dualistic; that is, it is ever in space-time. The Absolute or Consciousness, on the other hand, is fully intangible and unimaginable in the dualistic mode of functioning. Metaphorically speaking, there is an iron curtain that separates the two. Your idea of God or the Real is still a projection of ordinary, linear thought, and even your thesis that a face cannot be separated from its expression must itself be a play of that limited consciousness. An important breach exists, which can perhaps best be understood by analogy as the difference between one who is dreamlessly asleep and one who is part of the dream, ever sprouting new and old thought constructs. Never the twain shall meet!

To rephrase this, we may have intimations of what lies beyond the (ordinary) consciousness, but can never have actual knowledge of It, because that Beyond is simply unknowable. Anything to be known must be of the same structure and essential nature as the knower. Thus, whatever is known is a function of our limited thought, of what we are and do as a body-mind entity. To us, knowledge must ever remain a mere derivative of the Knowledge that is Unknowable, which lies in a different dimension.

V: Reading your book *Discovering the Realm Beyond Appearance* took me back to my deliberations about "reality." Since it became clear to me that we live in a consensus reality, a reality imposed on us by the society we live in, I came to the conclusion that I may as well accept it the way it's presented to me and live in harmony with my surroundings. This allowed me to live sanely within the context of this reality. I hereby leave aside the question of whether the society we live in is a sane one or not. Some so-called "primitive" people in the world have managed to develop techniques to shift their attention to a separate, equally valid reality consistent in its perceptions. This makes the quest for the ultimate reality an insurmountable task to me. Furthermore, it strikes me that any search is a self-centered activity, reinforcing the feeling of an entity doing the search. We have knowledge about the world, knowledge just being the act of naming things. This is a chair, that is a wall. I am depressed, you are enlightened, and so on.

We experience things in the world based on this knowledge. To directly experience something out there is something we cannot do. The something out there is something we will never be able to know. We just know the description of it. So where does all this leave me? It appears to me that any shift in a person is caused by a random occurrence.

We can talk about the non-existence of an "I" until we are blue in the face, and everything still stays the same. Those who are struck, at random it seems to me, are the lucky ones. There is no technique that can take you there. The technique of non-doing, the negative approach—not this, not that—is also a positive approach. There is the anticipation of something happening, which makes it a positive approach. At last I got the feeling that I was put in a double bind. Damned-if-I-do and damned-if-I-don't type of situation. Or a Catch-22 type of case. You do something, but there is always a catch that makes it impossible to attain the desired results.

RP: You are right! If one makes this into another system or technique—something that so many spiritual aspirants appear to do—you will miss. You will be merely repeating someone else's discovery.

The mind is a tired, old mechanism that can never lead to anything of value. So long as you strive for a result, you will miss. All the truly genuine teachings of non-duality aver this, and that is really all they state.

From directly talking to you, I know full well that you personally have gone beyond this stage of relative ignorance. The things you say are so true and cannot be repeated often enough. We need to die to the entire contents of consciousness, including all the methods and techniques to achieve this very same aim. The ultimate paradox!

V: I have a question about Nisargadatta Maharaj's book *I Am That*. He often suggests concentrating on "I Am," but at other times he says the notion of "I Am" is false. Have you any ideas about this?

RP: The very notion of the desirability of consistency is false. Any and every statement depends on so many variables and reference points that one may as well forget about such a yardstick. A statement does not only depend on the speaker, but also on the degree of understanding of his audience. Nisargadatta was once questioned on this very point; his answer was recorded in one of the books of dialogues. Unfortunately, I cannot retrieve the exact quotation but the gist of it was that if he were to talk to the villagers in the same manner as he did in Mumbai, they would lynch him.

So whenever he went into the country for talks, he adjusted his message to the people's degree of comprehension.

I would further say that we have made absolute consistency into an unrealistic ideal that may have its place in science, but not in something as fluid and intangible as spirituality. Linear thinking and logic are certainly important requisites in science and philosophy, but they operate strictly within the fields of thought and logic. And the latter inevitably lie about our real nature, which can only be hinted at since it is inexpressible.

V: What is the best way for one to deal with the fears and desires of the ego?

RP: There is no "best way." Nor can the ego be tempered. It can be extinguished—but only for a short moment. This may sound radical, but there is no possibility of negotiating with the ego, no way of tempering its pernicious activities. It is an either/or situation. Moreover, the ego cannot be killed once and for all; that is not how things work. The ego must and can be exposed from moment to moment, so that eternal vigilance is the watchword. In the full light of awareness, the ego collapses like a balloon pricked with a pin. But in a moment of unawareness, the ego is right back!

V: Is it better to work out one's past or simply drop it?

RP: Working out one's past is only a theoretical possibility, for it would take an infinite amount of time, like emptying the ocean with a bucket. In practice, it is a process to which there is no end.

To drop the past is not simply a passive activity. It requires a thorough investigation of what the ego is, how it comes about from moment to moment, and how it maintains itself. Essentially, the ego is only thought, based on the more or less enduring perception of a physical shape (the body), leading to an imprint called the "I" or "me," but essentially still only a particular configuration of thought. To cope with thought and not become victimized by its inherent tyranny requires constant vigilance. There is no shortcut in this endeavor. What is required is a life-long commitment to paying attention to one's thought process—something that few of us can or want to do.

V: Should one concentrate on positive character attributes such as faith, patience, love, etc. or should one just rise above all pairs of opposites?

RP: In the first instance it is good and helpful to foster those values that cater to communal rather than purely individual interests. Even if there is still a certain amount of confusion in this matter, it is worthwhile to make an effort in this. Now, to rise above all pairs of opposites is something entirely different; this is more a matter of maturity. Both approaches, being on different levels of reality, can coexist and do not necessarily stand in opposition. Naturally, to rise above all pairs of opposites is paramount, since it is only then that conflict may cease. But waiting until one succeeds might mean that one never gets down to taking in hand the mundane chores, problems, and confusions of everyday life. It is essential to create and maintain order as much as possible, both physically and, more importantly, mentally. While the house is on fire, immediate action is required, and one cannot wait until perfection is achieved. Every movement towards order in one's personal life will also enhance order in society. This, therefore, should be a high priority.

You raise the question of rising above all pairs of opposites, which has a nice ring to it but may essentially be unrealistic or utopian to wish for. The ego is a construct of thought, the source of all conflict, which, plainly put, equals the sphere of unreality, or *Maya*. Obviously, extinction of the ego is a noble endeavor. But who is going to do the extinguishing? By definition, it cannot be the ego. The body may commit suicide, but never the mind or the self. It can only happen seemingly spontaneously—that is, outside space and time, and therefore mysteriously, literally by itSelf, when a unique and unknown set of conditions prevails. For this to occur, it is said that what is needed is Grace, since it is beyond the ego's control; the ego does not and cannot enter into this at all. Should it happen against all odds, would it be a temporal or a permanent event? My sense is that it takes place in the moment and for the moment; that is, beyond space-time altogether.

This other level lies totally beyond any imaginable concept. It is verily the sourceless Source of everything—the Self (with a capital S). More accurately, it embraces or incorporates all levels of existence and lies beyond dimension. This Source or Self cannot be manipulated, for it is at once the Totality. Nor can it be understood intellectually, because that which would attempt to understand or control it subsists at a different level of existence. It overrides all temporal causes, cannot be defined in any manner, and operates by its own inscrutable laws. The ego can only surrender to the Self, recognize its false boundaries, created by Imagination, and be re-absorbed by its very Source—a very rare event.

V: It still amazes me how simple it all is! It is clear to me that I am not the body, the mind, or the senses. The world is within me, and there is no "person" here at all. Why we spend so much time trying to get to where we already are is baffling. Our conditioning from our so-called birth is indeed strong. Since that time, I have been integrating my understanding with everyday life, or at least trying to do so. I have found your recent book very helpful in this regard. I am noting that, as Sri Poonja suggests, reading books on *advaita* makes more sense after you know who you are, rather than before. As you suggest, "one's understanding should be honed and tested within one's own consciousness in everyday living. For most of us this is a lifelong activity." You also mentioned that Nisargadatta Maharaj stressed "courage" after proper understanding, and that it is necessary to really let go and live the teachings.

One of the things that is most interesting about seeing who you are (or what you are not) is that it is only the beginning. I had assumed previously that it would be the end of my search, that all my problems would be solved, and that would be the end of it. However, life goes on. I have friends and family to relate to, and basic mundane chores to attend to. I have various *vasanas* and *samskaras* that are still sticking around. Have you found this to be the case as well? Losing the body seems to be of little importance, and most of the time I see the mind's patterns, which sometimes produce a good laugh. I would appreciate any insights you may have regarding living with the Non-State. Few teachers of *advaita* seem to address this issue.

RP: On the latter subject in particular, I would like to make the following comments. True realization of one's essential nature does not eliminate one's worldly, everyday-life concerns, but places them in an entirely different perspective. Problems will persist, but the problem-maker has been transformed and takes a back seat to all the goings-on. The situation is difficult to put into words but is experiential. You will find yourself much more efficient at handling that part of your life. As Dr. D.T. Suzuki once expressed it, after *satori*, one walks a few inches above the ground.

In living in *advaita*, one is really dealing with an all-or-nothing situation. Letting go of the doer, one lets go of everything that the mind cherishes. The mind has been checkmated and can no longer interfere. Don't worry if it comes back—or tries to—all the time, even if one prides oneself on having overcome some great hurdle to spiritual progress. The enlightenment mechanism is like that of a switch: it is either on or off, and there is no in-between state.

V: The mind itself is the biggest problem. Defining and grasping are part of the mind's mechanisms for dealing with matters.

RP: We are hypnotized by the mind.

V: The mind is us.

RP: You can't pin down what we are. That which we use to pin it down is the mind again, so we are only going in circles. This makes us powerless, when in the ordinary way we try to get an answer with finality.

V: It is something.

RP: It is more than "something." It is beyond the wildest expectations of the mind. You can't use words . . . you fall silent. We are that silence.

V: One, I am the knower. Two, what is surrendering me is "me," the container . . .

RP: With these ideas, however, we are still dealing with the problem of the mind in more or less abstract terms. The manifold scattered impressions, the concepts, the fears and anticipations in their totality make up the mind. As soon as we say "our" or "my" mind, we already give sustenance to the erroneous idea of the ego or "I"-ness that we carry with us. For this conclusion is as unwarranted as taking a rainbow in the sky as a real entity, with an existence of its own.

What strengthens and gives continuity to the various thought processes that in toto make up the mind are always a preoccupation with the future. The future of what? The concerns of thought are ever with entities, presumed realities if you like, based on the body image. The mind's activity is unthinkable without the body entity one has embraced as oneself. Without the body, what is there to think, to do? Nothing. The mind has no more fuel in the "no-body" state, which is the state of death. We may take this state either literally as a dematerialized state of nothingness, or figuratively as a human entity totally devoid of self-importance. What this ultimately comes down to is the maintaining of the thought activity, with the identification of mind as a mental "me" in the reality of the body.

Ultimately, there would be no sustenance of the whole mental process without the presumed reality of the body, which lies at the root of the feeling of being a separate entity. All thought is concerned with the future state of the body. There is this constant movement from the past to the future, which is the mental process, and also the process of time. In its absence, we are in the present moment.

In the stillness of the Now, we are in full acceptance of what is; no longer concerned with the body, its presence, nor its absence. It might as well be dead. But all I normally do in my mental life is feed that physical entity, make it better, more "secure," etc.

At this point, right at the beginning of the sequence of mental processes, the question then arises as to the "reality" of the body—the ultimate starting point of the process of duality, of delusion. This we have done on numerous occasions in these meetings, and should be everyone's concern, either individually or when exploring together with others of similar interests and dispositions.

V: I have been digesting what you said in a recent meeting, and the impact of it is mounting within me like a snowball rolling down a hill. You describe the mind as a machine gone "amok" with a will of its own—or words to that effect. The image burns into my mind.

I haven't the slightest idea of who or what I am, but I am certain that there is nothing of me in the world except that I give the world reality. It is also clear that there is nothing whatsoever that can be done about any of this except to let this understanding work in consciousness.

Thank you for helping to set me straight in several areas of my confusion.

RP: What you say is absolutely correct. Even though some rocky road may still lie ahead, at least you're now pointed in the right direction!

You state: "I haven't the slightest idea of who or what I am. . . ." Yes, and nor does anyone else. In this realm, ideas or concepts do not apply at all; they cannot touch the purity of what you really are. Just *be* it. Any kind of "knowing" in the conventional sense, within a subject-object relationship, cannot refer to the Self. What you are as the Ultimate Subject is the background in which all your "knowing" takes place. So how could a fractional activity, such as perceiving or knowing—ever proceeding from a point of view, an ego—embrace the totality? Surely, if it were to take place, then such knowing of the background would need its own background to be known, and this sequence would have to repeat itself in an endless regression. Therefore, one would never be free from dualism. However, the moment the point of view disappears, you, as the background, glory in yourself as the only reality—the One without a second. This background is immutable; it is that which never changes and so itself is unaffected by desire and fear, nor does it undergo birth and death.

We all get a foretaste of the joy and bliss of this eternal state in the short periods before falling asleep and immediately upon waking; right after the satisfaction of a desire;

and in the interval between two thoughts. You then get an apperception, an intuition, of the Self before the whole array of mental constructs have yet appeared. These moments are especially precious; be fully aware of them, stabilize in them, but not through clinging, which immediately destroys the timeless dimension. Thus, rather than striving to be that Self—which is really absurd, for at any moment one cannot be anything but oneSelf—just be cognizant of the many false representations that thought has made of "oneself." Remaining aloof as the unaffected Witness, one bathes all these illusions or *Maya* in the pure light of awareness—the personality constructed by thought, the identification with that personality, the latter's nefarious activities—until all these accretions on the Self have dissolved and only the Awareness remains. This, in a nutshell, is the path of *jnana*, the knowing which is not-knowing.

A Tricky (or Trick?) Question

V: For several years I have been taking courses in philosophy and epistemology, in which the following question was asked either to trip us up or to wake us up: "Does a falling tree in a forest make any sound if there is no one around to hear it?"

RP: For some strange reason, people like to ask me this very same question, like setting a trap . . . [*laughter*].

I have heard this question answered by postulating that there is always some observer around, be it a passing animal, an insect, or whatever. While this answer is not incorrect, it is not entirely correct either.

First of all, the questioner might come back with: "Suppose there is not even one creature around to testify to the sound? Would there then be a silent forest?"

There is no need to wriggle out of it in this way. The right approach is to face the problem head-on and challenge the very foundations upon which it is based with some good, old-fashioned common sense: A "sound" is produced by virtually every process in nature, whether witnessed or not. In the case under examination, a pressure wave ensues upon the falling of the tree in the forest. This pressure wave may be considered to be an extension of the physical process of the falling tree. This pressure wave may or may not be translated into what we call "sound," depending on whether or not it is picked up by the appropriate equipment (which might be a biological ear or a mechanical one such as a microphone or other detector). The problem comes down to one of semantics: the correct understanding of what constitutes "sound" by transcending the meaning of that term. Here, we might postulate that any pressure wave is ipso facto a "sound," and whether it is picked up or not is irrelevant. The whole of the universe, the entire world process, is tantamount to one continuous sound. As you probably know, according to Hindu philosophy the universe was originally created out of sound, the "primordial sound," and it still is "sound." (Read this as "vibration." Quantum mechanics teaches that all fundamental particles are packages of energy—that is, vibration of one kind or another.) Thus: Yes, there is a sound but probably no one "listens" to it (in the narrow, accepted sense) in that "silent" forest. And no, the presence or absence of a "listener" does not concern us, and the dilemma implied in the supposedly tricky question falls flat on its face . . . or should I say, "on deaf ears"?

✢ ✢ ✢

Dear Dr. Powell,

It is not easy to find people interested in discussing spirituality, the teachings of J. Krishnamurti, etc., especially here in the middle of the Bible Belt. So after reading your books, which I found very enlightening, I thought I would drop you a line.

I have a question: Are there hints, glimpses of Truth? How much value should one attach to experiences? Krishnamurti states over and over again that you either live in Truth or you don't. To explain, I have had several "glimpses." I never try to go back to them, as Truth is in the present.

My first encounter with Krishnamurti occurred in 1952, while browsing through the Los Angeles Main Library. It was quite startling. Strange, how long it can take to shake off one's beliefs. One may do it, yet the self doesn't give up so easily. I have discovered that one must be aware at all times, since we slip back so easily. But whether or not I ever really see things as they are, it is good not to be encumbered by religious beliefs, or any beliefs for that matter.

Yours sincerely, M.

Dear Sir,

You wonder about the significance of your experiences, and ask if there is an intimation of truth. What am I to say? Only you can answer these questions, and are in a position to deal with them. What others say has no value, is irrelevant. To me, there is an intimation of Truth—but only to the Silent Mind, which, incidentally, is something else again: neither your mind, my mind, nor any "individual" entity. That Mind experiences, or rather is in a state of Truth: it is Truth.

Experiences come and go, and one goes along with them—naturally. One should neither encourage nor discourage experiences, unusual or otherwise. If one is just aware of them, one need not bother about anything. All that matters is not to be caught by them, or in any evaluation, which effectively blocks one from moving, from breaking through. Experiences are always of the past, never the actual, living Present. Life is this very movement, and one can only get on board if one has absolutely no baggage. By dropping all these preoccupations, seeing their irrelevance, one becomes very light, very free . . . nothing.

Yours sincerely, R.P.

⌗ ⌗ ⌗

Dear Mr. Powell,

I got your address through Editora Pensamento, here in São Paulo, on the assumption that you wouldn't mind this small intrusion. I hope that, as you read my letter, you will understand my anxiety in writing you, and will therefore forgive me.

I am 37 years old. Seven years ago, as I was going through frequent crises of anguish and anxiety, not knowing where to turn, I ended up on psychotherapy. I had been gradually losing the few interests I had in life, most of them artistic. The only unexplored field that was left was mysticism, from which I was constantly running away after having escaped from Catholicism. Deep inside me there was a kind of long-ing that didn't seem to suit all the movements, sects, and religions that I knew of. But I tried to suffocate this longing by giving myself over to pleasure, which, of course, was very easy.

Soon, I began to develop every kind of fear imaginable. All of a sudden, this young man who traveled a lot, led an agitated social and cultural life, drank constantly and had sex almost daily, couldn't even think of leaving town and kept himself at home most of the time, away from movies, bars, and even friends.

I didn't feel like a recluse, or like running away from the world; I merely felt that something was happening and it needed attention. I plunged myself into mystical literature and, since I kept finding them too moralistic for my taste, was told by my therapist about Krishnamurti. That was the end and the beginning.

I had no barriers for his message, and contact with his words can be considered as the most important thing that has ever occurred to me. I am sure you know what I am talk-ing about. After seven years, I still insist on finding people with whom I can talk about these incredible revelations that happen daily as we watch life, but it seems that people are becoming more blind and more deaf every day. I abandoned psychotherapy a few months later, but tried last year to get back into it, not as a therapy anymore, but as a way of discussing things with this man who had, after all, introduced me to K. However, it proved a failure. He is too interested in his analytical process and uses K. only for amusement. But now I feel the importance, the urgency, of standing alone and not running after people in search of discussions anymore. If life makes us meet, wonderful; if not, let it be so.

It happens that sometimes you need someone who speaks your language to expose things that you have found out, and try to understand them better. That is why I am writing you this letter. I might add that the reading of your books has come to me as a step forward on the way shown by Krishna-murti. And even though I feel, as I have said, that people are getting blinder and deafer every day, I also feel that the unmasking of the Ego has never been dealt with so seriously as in our time. Perhaps only in ancient India, China, and Japan, but that seems a long time ago, and when we think of all the confusion it created . . .

Thank you very much for your attention. If it is possible for you to answer my letter, I would be very happy. But if not, I would be happy all the same, and look for the answer in life itself.

Sincerely yours, N.

Dear Sir,

Thank you for your letter. Your background as described in it, and your experiments with different life styles that eventually led to your discovery of J. Krishnamurti, are not at all atypical. Also, your experience with psychotherapy fits into that same mold. It is good that you have traveled this route through actually experiencing these things for yourself, and not vicariously through hearsay, perhaps held back by moralistic considerations.

For me, Krishnamurti has been a milestone on life's journey. But only a way station, not the end of the line as far as probing spirituality is concerned. Circumstances have recently led me into getting involved with a modern Indian sage by the name of Sri Nisargadatta Maharaj (he died in 1981 at the age of 84) and to play a part in spreading his teachings in the West. If you wish to broaden and deepen your understanding of life, I urge you not to stop at K., but to continue to look for increased clarity in any direction that might help you. Maharaj took things a step further, although in a sense he is grounded in the traditional Hindu teachings but understands them in his own unique, totally non-traditional and irreverent way. Like Krishnamurti, he represented the complete rebel in a spiritually (and in other ways) moribund society. SNM, although considered a fully enlightened *jnani*, was a householder, married, with a family, and was during part of his life a small-business entrepreneur. There was no duality between his teaching and his personal lifestyle (and this is an area where there are some questions regarding K.).

With best wishes, yours sincerely, R.P.

⚜ ⚜ ⚜

Dear Mr. Powell,

Thank you for your kind reply. I was afraid you would not understand my letter, since it was written in quite a confused way. But, fortunately, it seems you had no great trouble with it. I have been playing with this matter of diseases, medicine, etc., these last few weeks and believe it has become much clearer now. What I meant to say was that, since everything that is put together by thought is intended to strengthen the Ego (which is of course thought itself), obviously our traditional view of medicine is also part of the same vicious circle: a diseased society produces a diseased medicine to take care of this same diseased society.

Therefore, its approach is typical of every action undertaken by thought; that is, identifying, labeling, taking action. This attack on the so-called "virus" is what seems to me to be the greatest disaster of all. I cannot understand a murderous force being born out of this wondrous harmony that is the world we live in. We are the creators of disharmony. What if these "viruses" (which have been accepted as such for a long time without being really challenged) are a way of life itself trying to re-harmonize the organism that is sick? What if the incredibly fast evolution of these beings is life itself desperately fighting our medicines to try and save the diseased body?

The doctors, imposing their therapies on the patient (who gives himself up completely to the doctor's mandate), are obstructing the way of Nature's self-healing mechanism and therefore condemning the patient to death. We end up always getting the same warning sign that reads. "Pay attention to every step you take and make sure not to fall into the traps prepared by thought." For me, words are the trap. I always ask myself how things were before the advent of words. We never seem to see that the human being was not born with a dictionary by his side. . . .

If I don't put a label on a strange sensation that I feel, I'm sure that being attentive to it, I would open the doors to whatever way is needed by Nature so that it can work on what seems to be wrong and heal it (or not). If the defensive way we adopt against life, psychologically speaking, is in itself our destruction, the same can be said regarding medicine, which is, along with psychology, etc., a creation of thought.

Thank you very much for your kind attention, N.

Dear Sir,

Thank you very much for your reply. Yes, of course, what you state is correct: ". . . our traditional view of medicine is also part of the same vicious cycle: a diseased society produces a diseased medicine to take care of this same diseased society." But we must also realize that this same unhealthy mindset produces an excessive and therefore unhealthy preoccupation with ill health and a glorification of so-called physical fitness. And underlying all this is, of course, our fear of death and the fact that we have been unable to come to grips with this issue.

With respect to viruses, etc., you are raising some very deep and interesting issues that have scarcely been explored. However, my knowledge in this field is insufficient for me to make pertinent comments. I don't like to speculate or talk about things that lie outside my ken. One thing I would say, however, is that nature does not seem to care a damn whether or not the individual creature survives. "Nature," as an abstraction, seems only to strive for the survival of the species, and then only within the context of a general "balance of nature."

I can say with certainty that the mind plays a much bigger part in the creation of disease and dis-ease (and therefore also in their cure) than generally credited by the orthodoxy. Our lack of understanding in this connection is due to our artificial and incorrect splitting of body and mind as two distinct realms. A holistic view is therefore highly desirable, if not essential, in finding lasting cures of disease. The way I view this disease-causing process is that certain faulty thought-habits, loaded with contradiction, conflict, and "unnatural" emotion, cause psychological stress and corresponding pathological changes on the muscular and cellular levels of the individual. These somatic changes are probably mainly caused by disruption in the flow of *prana*, or vital energy through the body, just like an organ that receives an insufficient blood supply, and therefore insufficient nutrition, fails in its function.

You are right that "words are the traps." This, as you well know, is one of the main pillars of K.'s teaching. But when you further ask how things were before the advent of words, you are already talking purely the language of Nisargadatta, even though you have never heard of him. Nisargadatta always asks what is prior to mind and prior to words. The following quote (from *I Am That*) sums it up beautifully:

"The moment you start talking you create a verbal universe, a universe of words, ideas, concepts and abstractions, interwoven and interdependent, most wonderfully generating, supporting and explaining each other and yet all without essence or substance, mere creations of the mind. Words create words, reality is silent."

To the question, "If words have no reality in them, why talk at all?" he responded: "They serve their limited purpose of interpersonal communication. Words do not convey facts, they signal them. Once you are beyond the person, you need no words."

Finally, "The mind shapes the language and the language shapes the mind. Both are tools, use them but don't misuse them."

With kind regards, R.P.

⊕ ⊕ ⊕

Dear Mr. Powell,

I would appreciate any reply you could give me to the following questions.

1. I find Maharaj to sound somewhat intolerant of his guests, as well as slightly defensive. For example, on page 61

of *The Nectar of Immortality:* "I am going to send you out of here. . . ." Why is he exhibiting such impatience, or am I misreading the passage?

2. I wish to pose questions regarding the body-mind phenomena. M. seems to disregard them. The reality is "I Am" and I possess a body—why reject it? Why not play along with the *Maya?* I wish to understand the phenomena of healing, trance channeling, visualization, and manifestation. Can you elucidate these? Are these valid experiences or not? M. talked about miracles not as something that one has control over, but rather as something spontaneous and uninitiated by Beingness. Do I understand this correctly?

3. Maharaj says that "experiencing the Absolute while having the Beingness is between the sleep and waking state." The brain wave pattern then is between *beta* and *theta*—the supposedly *alpha* state. If one induces an *alpha* brain wave pattern, can one then experience the Absolute and be conscious of it? And what is the phenomenon of out-of-body experience as authored by Robert Monroe?

4. On page 108 of *Nectar:* Maharaj says "of all the species, the most evolved is the human being." What evolves? The five basic elements, or the mind flow? Can you answer this important question please? Also, page 82 reads: "These words carried a profound meaning and I felt that he was

spiritually quite an advance soul." Please tell me what an advanced soul is, according to Maharaj.

5. On the top of page 81 of *Nectar:* "But the witness of the Consciousness is the highest principle—the Absolute." Does this statement imply that there could be information from the Absolute filtering through Universal Consciousness to the body-mind? If so, is this what is referred to as "channeling"?

6. On page 111 of *Nectar:* M. refers to the traditional order of the Nine Gurus and the power of the sacred name. Who and what are these? Please explain.

7. On page 6 of *Nectar:* The *parabrahman* state is defined as eight days prior to conception. Please, what defines the other seven days prior to conception? If Beingness is the outcome of food, then if one varies the type of food eaten, can one affect one's state of consciousness or level of knowingness? Please explain.

8. On page 76 of *Seeds of Consciousness:* "'The personal entity 'you' is watched." This statement assumes that "you" the Absolute is doing the watching. However, it was stated by M. that the Absolute is impersonal and has no attributes. I find this contradictory. Also, on pages 45 and 180 of *Seeds,* M. makes statements regarding rebirth that seem directly contradictory.

I consider these questions very important. I am quite serious in my endeavors. I would appreciate so much in hearing from you. Thank you for the opportunity to write to you.

Sincerely, K.R.

Dear Miss R.,

In reply to your letter of 28 February, I have attempted to clarify your questions and comments as follows:

1. Maharaj often jostles his visitors. Some of these people come for reasons other than acquiring knowledge (e.g., to score in a verbal skirmish). M. sees through such people quickly. Besides, space in his abode is at a premium, and he feels that everyone should have a chance to attend the sessions.

2. You misread M. here. M. does not reject body-mind and its phenomena; he rejects only one's identification with it. Thus, it is valid to say "I possess a body," but it is not valid to say "I am that body."

You write: "Why not play along with the *Maya?*" That's exactly what M. suggests: to go along with it, because one understands its unreality. The error that almost everybody makes is to take it seriously and get involved with it.

Regarding the phenomena you mentioned, M. rarely comments on these, as he considers them irrelevant for the *sadhaka.* Sometimes he refers visitors to gurus known for their prowess in *siddhis,* such as Sai-Baba, Muktananda, and so on. In *I Am That,* M. refers to certain powers that can be cultivated by appropriate training. All spiritual teachers, however, stress that *siddhis* can be a dangerous distraction in which one can easily get lost. Insofar as they occur spontaneously as a by-product of one's spiritual development, they are best ignored since they have no particular spiritual value. On the other hand, their conscious cultivation may well be a ploy by the ego to boost itself.

3. M.'s reference to "experiencing the Absolute" is not and cannot be that of the dualistic experience, requiring a subject and object. "Experiencing" here means *being* the Absolute. One ever is the Absolute, but we have not woken up to that fact. In the transition from the waking to the sleep state, at the instant the "I-am-ness" subsides, in that timeless moment, M. maintains, it is possible to know that we are purely the Absolute. At that point, the *Maya* state drops away, and we enter another state.

As to "experiencing the Absolute" through inducing an *alpha* brain wave pattern, this seems to me an inherently contradictory, unstable mode. What or who is the inducing agent? The ego or mind, of course. So whatever results can only be an unstable condition. Better to empty the mind, dispel all illusion, and simply be what remains: the Emptiness that we may call the Absolute.

4. The human species is the most evolved in the sense that it possesses the greatest potential to be conscious of itself, to know itself, and to transcend its time-bound state. Of course, all this has come about through the play of the five elements and the three *gunas*. The five elements themselves do not evolve; they are primary, gross elements, but through their endless combinations and permutations with the *gunas*, different kinds of food bodies "evolve." As M. would say, the quintessences of the food bodies give rise to creatures with varying levels of consciousness, while the indwelling principle is unvarying, having neither color nor design.

What is it that evolves? Only the bodily form (i.e., bodily parameters such as posture, central nervous system, cortex, etc.). As I stated before, the indwelling principle remains the same, but expresses itself differently, according to the bodily form.

The mind flow does not evolve; it is a secondary parameter, and is related to bodily form and sensory impressions. The thoughts forming the mind flow are reactions to impressions from the outside, and these reactions depend on the constitution of the sensory mechanism. The mind flow is a purely mechanical process, dependent on impressions *(samskaras)*.

What does M. mean by his saying that "he was spiritually quite an advanced soul"? This is simply a colloquial expression for "a person with a very deep understanding of spiritual matters." As you must well realize, M. does not hold to the Christian concept of "soul" and its so-called advancement.

5. The answer to your question must be "no." The most refined manifestation of the Absolute is "witnessing." The Absolute itself, not having any attributes, is prior to Consciousness and therefore prior to Knowledge or Information. Channeling, and all such processes are part of the *Maya*.

6. For this, see the footnote on page 15 of my book, *The Blissful Life.*

As M. explains, *nama-japa* may be useful for beginners to break the identification with name and form. In this connection, the spiritual name adopted may act as a constant reminder of one's real nature.

7. The "eight days" is merely a shorthand for any period prior to conception. Elsewhere, M. talks about a month, and so on. There is no particular significance to his use of the number eight.

8. The answer is "yes." It has long been a tenet of Hinduism that the type of food one consumes influences one's consciousness. Hence, they talk about *sattvic* food, *rajasic* food, etc. Generally, a *sattvic* diet is held to be most beneficial— that is, vegetarian and bland foods, no onions, no spices, etc.

Maharaj himself did not restrict himself to such foods—he was not even a vegetarian. Obviously, he does not consider such a diet mandatory for one's spiritual development.

I am somewhat hesitant to comment on statements made in *Seeds of Consciousness* and *Prior to Consciousness,* because I have some inside information on the difficulties experienced as Jean Dunn was editing these books, such that one can never be entirely sure of their accuracy. I will say, however, that on the face of it, M. makes indeed contradictory statements about reincarnation, among other things. I can easily explain that to you. You see, the books are records of private discussions with individuals having different backgrounds and degrees of comprehension. They were not primarily intended to be published in book form. So, with beginners, M. goes along with their various simple beliefs, including that of reincarnation. With more advanced students, M. is ruthlessly outspoken. Furthermore, this issue of reincarnation is actually a secondary one. If we understand the teaching as a whole, and particularly the question "Who Am I?," then reincarnation no longer has any relevance; we see through the matter, and that is the end of it. For this reason M., in the final stage of his life, was increasingly reluctant to even discuss this issue.

Trusting that these notes will be of some help to you in your quest,

Yours sincerely, R.P.

# # #

Dear Sir,

Having read your book on Zen, one thing strikes me right away when looking at my life and comparing to others in this respect: when thoughts flow through my head rapidly like a young mountain stream, I am happy, but when I hold on to things like an old and sluggish river meandering down to the sea, I am unhappy; constant change makes me happy, and to be surrounded by this society that is so out of touch with me and therefore I with it, creates constant conflict. I would be happy to be lost in eternal bliss, pumping out my waste thoughts and bodily waste at a series of brooks, rather than be stuck in a society that hounds me into submission at every possible chance. (I do not fit in here and am glad to be what I am, but I am not happy with the persecution, based on jealousy, thrown continually my way and disturbing my peace of mind.)

I know now how Jesus, John F. Kennedy, or anyone else feels who stands pat in any field of endeavor and says, "stop hugging the past (objective reality) and reach out for the future." True happiness is the journey not the arrival, the attempt not the achievement, the competition not the prize. Life is movement, stagnation is death.

People fear for their jobs because they are not willing to learn something new, to change their lives of boring, mindless repetition, which acts like a mantra, blocking out all awareness, like radar jamming. Ritual blinds people to the truth, as does untested but believed-in superstition.

Science says that physically, we start dying from birth—spiritually that's true also. The contrast of the great Void and this reality (as you call it) is such that only analysis of the minor details of life keeps adults alive. Children adjust to the staggering differences between the two, which is why they seem overwhelmed and unable to cope.

Life isn't complex unless you are lost in the details (Gordian knot) or are trying to deceive others with regard to controlling them, in which case you claim it as your excuse for doing nothing.

Well, that's enough mental excreta caused by "eating" your book.

Yours sincerely, T.

Dear Friend,

My advice to you is very simple. Stay right where you are. Wherever you find yourself, it is the same stupid, non-understanding society. I know, I have traveled widely. Here in America, it might be a bit worse than in the U.K. But the real point is that any gallivanting around may hinder you from going deeply within yourself. Geography is totally irrelevant. When you really explore, you are no longer concerned with all these external things. Don't waste your time with them. There is no "external" as opposed to "internal." All is your Self. I cannot tell you more in a short letter.

Read the recommended books, including Sri Nisargadatta's. Don't be held back by anything. Don't even get "hung-up" on J. Krishnamurti. Become your own teacher.

Best of luck, R.P.

⁂ ⁂ ⁂

Dear Dr. Powell,

I am pleased to have made contact with you, and I appreciate your willingness to offer some guidance with regard to the teachings of Sri Nisargadatta Maharaj. First, let me offer some background information that may be useful to you.

In 1971 at the age of 20, I had a realization of who I am, which for all practical purposes, happened spontaneously. During this experience, I ceased to identify with the body and recognized myself as the timeless, formless awareness that was never born. When I looked at others, I saw myself in the sentience reflected through their eyes. After twenty-four hours, this realization left as spontaneously as it had arrived, and even though I knew the truth, I knew it as a memory and not living truth. Needless to say, I was deeply depressed and remained so for many years. About that time, I began practicing Transcendental Meditation (TM) as taught by Maharishi Yogi, and although I had several interesting experiences over the years, and fairly regular "deep" meditation, I never seemed to reconnect to my real Self. I continued to meditate regularly, and gradually the depression lifted and my life went on. I matured, married, became established in business, and was apparently successful. But deep inside, I felt separated from my real Self.

About ten months ago, I was introduced to *I Am That*, and the power of Maharaj's words has seemingly caused an explosive quickening of the process of transformation of consciousness. I understand a lot of what Maharaj says, directly from my own realization. My only problem is I have no one to discuss this with and am longing for some kind of confirmation of what is happening to me. If you will bear with me, I would like to explain what I've learned, and distinguish between that which is known to me through experience and that which is known intuitively. I may use words such as "see" and "experience" or "know," even though I realize that these realities may not be knowable in any formal sense. Trust me that I am talking about direct cognitive experience and not intellectual conceptualization.

I can see clearly that everything having a form cannot be real in any eternal sense. Likewise for anything having a beginning or an end. Thus, the real is beyond the world and beyond the mind.

Often in meditation (and also outside it while engaged in activity), I let go of all manipulations and experience what is really there, which has no qualities at all, but definitely *is*. Even though the real is without qualities, the mind and body register bliss, wholeness, warmth, at-one-ness, etc., when appreciating this reality. In other words, I seem to be appreciating my deepest Self—pure "is-ness" or Being, while at the same time the mind is having thoughts. While in this state, the thoughts are very profound and pure, and I can clearly see the thoughts as separate from reality itself, which stands apart as the silent screen on which the thoughts are displayed. I have assumed that this experience is the first stage of transcendence wherein the "I Am" is realized. Can you confirm?

This leads to a question about practice. Maharaj advises us to abide in the "I Am" as often as possible, and that consciousness will do the rest. I assume this to mean that the second stage of transcendence will happen spontaneously when consciousness is sufficiently prepared to shift from identification with form to identification with the formless. Therefore, other than establishing oneself in the "I am" or pure consciousness, there is nothing more to do—no more skill ever need exist. If this is the case, how is one to practice?

I meditate for two hours a day in three separate sittings. During this time, I am usually graced with several periods (ten minutes or so) in the state mentioned above. I have assumed it is not prudent to try to be in this state outside of meditation because it seems unnatural to force or manipulate the mind. If the state arises spontaneously while in activity, I enjoy it but do not seek it outside of meditation. From your study, do you think Maharaj would agree with this approach? My guiding principle has been to go with what seems natural, without force or effort. When in doubt, just be easy with what is.

On rare occasions (four or five times over the last year) I have felt my consciousness literally turned inside out, and I have become the Great One—the context (pure and abstract) for all that is. The world is in the mind, and both are inside of me. When this has happened, my individual mind has become profoundly frightened, and I am overwhelmed with fear of death or insanity. It is as if my mind says, "No way are you going to get me to go in there; I can't handle infinity. I'll break apart and you'll go mad." After a few days my fear seems to dissipate, but the experience leaves me wondering how it is ever possible to become realized in any full and final way. I have to assume that this is just a stage that we naturally transcend as consciousness gradually disassociates from the mind. Do you have any advice on this fear experience and how to get through it?

Finally, why and how is it that I can have these experiences, and yet they come and go? Is this normal? When I realize the reality, it is a living truth. Then it passes and it is a concept and a memory. Why does it leave? What are the mechanics of enlightenment? What is holding back the process? If enlightenment is sudden, why does it seem to be a gradual thing with me?

I thank you for listening to me, and would appreciate any insight or comments you can offer. Likewise, I would like to know of any students of Maharaj who are fully realized, whether that be you or someone else. I feel the need to discuss these matters in person with anyone who can genuinely be my guide.

Thank you for your attention,
Sincerely, S.

Dear Sir,

In reply to your letter of February 14, the following observations may possibly be of some relevance and use. It is a well-known fact that some individuals on more or less rare occasions experience moments of at-one-ness and peace with their environment, which could be a foretaste of total

union with reality. Such experiences usually occur spontaneously and uninvitedly, as it were. They can be all the more
remarkable and valuable if they occur at a tender age, before
the individual has been exposed to all sorts of religious and
philosophical teachings, and before he has imbibed all the
lies that society wishes to feed him. Then we know for certain
they are not the result of conditioning or projections of the
mind, or of any conscious effort to elicit such experiences.
They are for the most part intimations of a different way of
functioning, which stems from our natural state of being.

There is, however, a shadow side to the phenomenon,
which could make it into a double-edged sword. You see,
the experience is accompanied by varying degrees of understanding, ranging all the way from zero to full illumination.
The latter is extremely rare; we know of at least one such
case: Sri Ramana Maharshi as a young boy underwent a total
transformation immediately after his remarkable and now
legendary "death experience."

For most of us there needs to be a development of the
incomplete understanding that accompanies the experience.
We will want to repeat it again and again, for the very delight
it has given us, but this very wanting will only add to our
bondage. This is why the experience in itself does not signify
anything; indeed, it strengthens the mind with its thought

process, and keeps us from going beyond. What matters only is the depth of understanding. You seem already well aware of this problem, since you differentiate between "that which is known to me through experience and that which is known intuitively." Indeed, "intuition" is mankind's highest faculty for acquiring knowledge or *jnana*. It goes far beyond a mere intellectual understanding, which is still dualistic, since it is a play of concepts and implies a subject and an object.

Jnana is to be had primarily through inquiry. Hence, my advice is to stop dwelling on these experiences, which are mere memories and keep you bound to the sphere of space and time. This may be difficult at first, but will become easier upon seeing the irrelevance and actual hindrance that experience represents, and the overwhelming need for understanding the "experiencer." As Sri Nisargadatta Maharaj has stated, "Understanding is everything"; therefore, if one can come to that, nothing else needs to be done.

How do we deepen our understanding? Sri Nisargadatta, as you write in your letter, states that one should stay in the "I am" state as often as possible. That is easier said than done, as our first impulse is to repeat our self-encounter by an effort of will. Here the question is: Can the pure "I am" state be induced by any effort at all? If it is achieved through direct, positive effort, then it is a question of exerting one's "will." But is will not the sole territory of the mind? Does it not anchor me more firmly within the realm of time and space, which cannot offer any release? Maharaj must have meant more than this.

This is where we need meditation, but not the type of meditation based on performing certain disciplines or exercises, such as TM. The latter can be useful but are also a doubled-edged sword, as I will try to explain. The "good" thing about them is that they can quiet the mind and slow down the hectic thought process to some extent. For certain individuals, they are a prescribed provisional course of action, before they can even consider the more serious type of meditation. The other side of the coin is that most people who have felt the undoubted benefit of stilling the mind by doing this kind of *sadhana,* will stop at that and think that is all there is to it. They will get "stuck," psychologically and spiritually. The fact is that a becalmed mind is only the starting point, and a necessary one, on the spiritual journey. Realization is something completely different and not so easy to come by.

One must approach the "I am" state differently. It is just being oneself, free from psychological pressures, without any form of "becoming." After all, it is the most natural state of being and functioning. We are always ourselves only, but do not feel it that way because the mind has led us astray and coaxed us into accepting all sorts of false concepts about ourselves. Thus, we have misidentified our Self. The task therefore is to wipe away the entire mental superstructure, so that what is left only is the pure Self without superimpositions. In this enterprise one begins by exposing one's areas of confusion, especially the many contradictions, and other forms of mental blockage.

You state that occasionally your consciousness becomes all-embracing, yet at the same time "profoundly frightened" and "overwhelmed with fear of death or insanity." I have to tell you that this is not a meaningful stage in one's inquiry. Please see the contradiction in all this. What you experience as becoming the Great One can only be a projection by the mind. For if Oneness truly had been reached, there would be no fright because there is no longer an entity to be frightened. Along the same lines, there can be no fear of death because the latter comes only as the result of certain identifications. Believe me, although physically, the survival instinct remains intact, psychologically, the fear of death vanishes completely at a certain stage of one's meditation. But you must go much deeper; for instance, how can you be so certain that you were born? If you say, "yes," do you have this from your own experience (when and how?) or from hearsay? And if you say "yes," what is it that was born? If you still say "yes," then you bring into being a beginning point, and so the concept of "time." Do you understand what time is, and do you see that time is a product of memory and so a function of body-mind? If you truly go beyond body-mind, then what is left of time? I suggest these as primary topics for your inquiry; to contemplate these issues until they have become crystal clear. Then, as Maharaj said, Consciousness will do the rest.

You will find that there come stages of clarity, when the web of illusion, the *Maya* of our existence, which we ourselves have spun, is fully exposed and we are truly ourselves for a moment—"I am" in its purity. Your practice should be not to try to induce a repetition, but when the obfuscation of that clarity occurs, to contemplate that alone. Do not carry on with the memory of something that is not there anymore. Since realization is living totally in the present, you will never get there by cherishing memories. At such moments especially, inquire into the questions "Who am I?" and "Who is it that suffers?" See that the false "I" or ego has come about through identification not only with the body, but more importantly, through psychological identification with various kinds of mental constructs, which are all in reality pure imagination. I suggest you be very persistent in the latter activity; each time you feel some resistance in the natural flow of things, examine the underlying mental conceptualization, and expose the false identity that claims to be the "me"—the "doer" and the "experiencer." The power of discriminating awareness destroys the bubble of false identifications in the instant. In this way, you pierce through that which is illusory and not the "I am," rather than trying to hold on to the "I am." Understand that the "I am" cannot be controlled, but It controls everything.

Now, does this kind of meditation require set periods of sitting, or is it something that can happen at any time and all the time? While you are working, eating, or doing nothing in particular, there is a parallel activity taking place without any effort on your part.

When all is said and done, we must not forget that realization cannot be attained through hot pursuit, as we do in our worldly activities. It needs total surrender, a total divorce from the body-mind entity after one has realized that the entity is totally mechanical—it acts like a super-clever computer—and so has a life of its own that cannot be manipulated. (Who is to do it?) But this no longer matters because we definitely are not that entity. Ultimately, what we can do only is open ourselves so that Grace may befall us. For remember, without Grace nothing can be done, and with Grace everything is possible.

Regarding your question about stages of transcendence, I will answer by putting into words that which is beyond all words, and therefore is intended only for the purpose of elucidation. In actual fact, full transcendence can take place all at once, but this varies with the individual and with the depth of understanding. In most cases, this understanding needs some time to mature. Remember, it took Maharaj three years to fully develop this understanding, after receiving instructions in meditation from his guru.

Finally, you queried whether certain persons were fully realized. If I gave you the answer, what good would it do you? If the question was asked out of curiosity, it would only feed the mind and thus encumber your own process of emancipation. If it is with a view toward getting some encouragement, or even a "guarantee" for the teachings, it would again defeat the purpose, for encouragement is only building up the ego and so is fatal to the quest. Instead, investigate whether there is a "person" at all.

Realization is neither to be invited nor does it come as an award for one's "doing." Nor is there any guarantee that it must come at all, even with all one's "doings" and meditations; it is not up to the individual to determine that. Find out to whom all this is happening, who is "meditating"! Lead a normal life and do not try to become somebody. In realization, one is absolutely nothing; one disappears, as it were, from the face of the Earth! Do only what you can to destroy all illusion, and leave the rest to that Greater Power, which manifests itself to the individual as "Grace."

Please let me know of your progress.

Sincerely, R.P.

❋ ❋ ❋

Dear Mr. Powell,

I am sorry to tell you that I wasn't at all convinced by the word of the Maharaj. I found it full of contradictions, especially where exercises, practicing, meditation, and rituals are concerned. You see, Krishnamurti showed us so clearly that everything that is created by thought cannot lead to Truth. I feel this so deeply that the simple mention of self-imposed practices makes me turn away. I see it today as complete nonsense.

Nisargadatta's language (at least through reading) seemed aggressive, and I missed that infinite sense of compassion that K.'s message possesses. It is not a matter of comparing the two, but since K. remains to me at least, the most objective, clear, simple, humble, and cohesive of all philosophers I have read, it is a situation difficult to avoid.

I understand that the Maharaj means a lot to you, but I am sure you will agree that on these matters you have to be deeply hit, and I wasn't. How can one be a revolutionary, while fixed in tradition?

I send you my best regards, N.

Dear N.,

I feel you are giving up on Nisargadatta a little too soon. Maharaj, too, was a revolutionary who had little or no time for orthodoxy. This will come out particularly clearly in a new book that I have just finished editing. (I suspect that certain things were left out of *Nectar of Immortality* by the devotees who forwarded me the manuscript; the new work is based directly on tapes of the meetings, which I transcribed.) Maharaj addressed different audiences according to their level of understanding; this accounts for the apparent contradictions. Maharaj also saw quite clearly the futility of all self-imposed practices; he would completely agree with you on that point. This is also brought out quite clearly in the new work.

His language may seem aggressive, but he was not one who suffered fools gladly. In this respect, it would be a mistake to take K., or anyone else for that matter, as "standard."

Yes, Maharaj means a lot to me, as you say, but not as a personality or master per se, but for the message. From that point of view, every master (and actually everything) that expresses the Ultimate is glorious and meaningful. As far as modern masters to whom I am indebted, I should mention also Ramana Maharshi and Krishna Menon (Sri Atmananda), whom I hold in as equally high esteem as Nisargadatta. I feel it is important to be a devotee of the truth rather than of a particular mouthpiece of that truth.

Krishnamurti has been helpful to me, too, but primarily in the beginning. As a psychological teaching, it is indeed supreme, but this is a mere stepping stone for one who is on the spiritual path. In the Introduction to a new book *(Path without Form: A Journey into the Realm Beyond Thought),* I have gone into the relationship between K. and the great *advaitic* masters somewhat more fully.

Talking about contradictions, have you read Mary Lutyens' third volume of the K. biography, *The Open Door?* This shows you another, more private side to K.'s "personality," which may be disconcerting to many of his devotees. All of this shows once again the need to remain detached from any individuality in the world, however great or famous. But that is difficult for people: since everyone sees himself as an individual, he automatically sees everyone else as a person, too.

With best wishes and regards, R.P.

⚓ ⚓ ⚓

Robert,

Nisargadatta Maharaj's talk on December 12, 1987, about what he says to the "thoughts" helped me very much. It made me realize that even Maharaj had huge tidal waves of thought hit him. I realize that I should not get so discouraged and feel failure so deeply.

Do you have any further material on this subject?

Thank you for your friendship, E.

Dear E.,

Thank you for your kind letter. No, I do not possess any new texts specifically dealing with the "Void." Even if I did, I don't think they would help you at all. At best, they would give only temporary relief. You see, any exclusive assault on the Void is bound to fail. We make peace with it only by embracing the Totality; that is, by allowing life's events to unfold with complete acceptance or letting-go. As long as we see the Void as something apart from ourselves, it is bound to induce fear and pain. The inevitability of this should be clear.

Then, ask yourself: Is the observer of the Void not also himself part of the Void? Think of the Void as the Observer without resistance, as in the blissful state of dreamless sleep, or as "you" were years (or maybe only days or minutes) ago in a care-free mood of "forgetfulness," however short-lived it may have been. Think of "you" as an infant innocent of the ways of the world, literally not knowing anything yet. Then go back still further, as That upon which the I-amness or Beingness descended uninvited and spontaneously. Abide in That only, and bypass the overlay of *Maya*—the "noise" of body-mind machinery—which is not your true Self. While abiding in your true Self, be aware of the "distractions," but do not act upon them. That overlay, all the knowledge of self-image and its relationships, is pure conditioning imposed on what you really are. It is only mental luggage, made of memories and hearsay, which we carry through life, and is our basic Ignorance. Happily, this luggage is only "acquired" and not innate. Just as you have acquired it, you can lose or discard it, when you see it for what it is and do not take it too seriously.

That dear E., should be your *sadhana,* as personally recommended by your friend,

Robert

\# \# \#

Dear Sir,

I have read several of your books and have enjoyed them thoroughly. You certainly have a unique grasp of J. Krishnamurti and Zen. This, I might add, is a neat trick, so to speak, as the former has been so misunderstood. He has been described by so-called knowledgeable people as an Eastern philosopher, which is altogether wrong. Even Needleman in his *New Religions* misses the mark occasionally.

At times you get a little too scientific for me. My mind simply doesn't work like that; it seems to just tune out in that particular dimension. For example, I took two mandatory courses in math at the university, and received a D in both—for showing up, I suppose—because I didn't have a clue as to what they were talking about. My mind simply refuses to follow any form of empirical logic, which in fact was a source of great pain in earlier years, as doors were closed that I wanted open. In retrospect, I realize how fortunate I was that they were not opened.

Once in the past, at a particularly dark moment in my life, I went to the library and started reading Krishnamurti. I began thinking, or rather feeling, with all my being: I must understand this man—I must! Then a voice suddenly said to me, out of the blue, as it were: "It is not this man that you must understand." I sort of floated out of the place—and this after reading Krishnamurti for years. It was so eminently simple. Yet, it is remarkable how deeply conditioned we are, to the extent that we can't see something that's right there before our eyes.

Regarding your books again, I have some difficulty with your equating "choiceless awareness" with "I am That," since the latter implies identification with something, or rather presents the question: Who is what? Of course, I realize these are just words posited by the intellect perhaps, but this interests me nonetheless. The intellect is forever asking questions that have no answers. Technological questions have answers, and this expectation of an answer somehow spills over into the psychological field. It is totally inappropriate, but thought does not see this. This basic error occurred at the beginning, or perhaps at some point in time, after thought had created "time" in the psychological sense. But I am beginning to speculate. I did enjoy Krishnamurti's discussions with David Bohm. I could not follow them intellectually, but there was sort of a deep thrill that I can in no way explain.

The position that all is illusion poses a difficulty for me. I realize it's all a matter of what is perceived, or rather the interpretation of what is perceived—like a horse galloping down a path aware of the trees running towards him, if he is not fitted with blinders. The fact that we are in a relative state of illusion is, as K. puts it, small consolation for one who has a toothache.

It does not require great wisdom to see that our lives are

in disorder. What requires wisdom is to resist the temptation to project an imaginary concept of order, or state of order, and try to approximate that image, rather than turn our attention to the disorder, and understand it, or simply see it as a fact: the "what is," for which seeing is the only thing necessary. It is its own action—the seeing—and there is no necessity for anything apart from it to act on, since there is nothing apart from it to act. Gosh, it takes a finely tuned something (which is no thing) to see this!

How terribly painful it is to go down this path. It brings to mind years ago when I was very much into theosophy. I picked up a book called *Candles in the Sun.* I could not finish the book, it was so shattering. I put it down and it was quite some time before I picked it up again and finished reading it. I was catapulted into other dimensions—not themselves without pain, but indeed without pat answers demanded by the intellect. These dimensions held intimations of that mystery that lies deep inside of us that we can thrill to feel—an immensity that transcends the dualistic demons of hope and despair.

Sincerely, J.B.

Dear Mr. B.,

Thank you for your open, sincere letter. You seem to possess the virtue of unpretentiousness—a plus in spirituality.

You hit the nail right on the head by stating that what matters is knowing oneself, not Krishnamurti. Also, the man and his teaching are two different things, and it is highly dangerous to have a fixation on, or idealize, the teacher—there is always the chance he might not turn out exactly as fantasized or idealized.

Your stated difficulty with science does not matter in the least. You see, there is room for different approaches, since we are dealing with individuals of all types. My apparently scientific or philosophic detours are aimed at those types who are particularly wedded to this kind of intellectual, conceptual thinking. It is meant to lead them to the inevitable paradox awaiting them in the end, and the realization that the discursive intellect is impotent and irrelevant in the search for self. From your letter I gather that you are more "heart-oriented" than "head-oriented," and so I can come straight to the point without such detours.

Let me try to clear up this question of choiceless awareness. We become acutely aware that there are no absolute values; that whatever we appear to be is nothing but concept, conditioning. Hence, there is no point in judging, approving or disapproving, approximating ourselves to an ideal, or clinging to anything. We perceive everything with full acceptance, choicelessly, for there is no longer any process of comparison with fixed standards of what "ought to be." The mind has fallen silent in total letting-go. If we pursue this to the very end, we realize our Emptiness or Nothingness, and that one is, and everything else is, a superimposition by the unreal, or *Maya*.

With respect to the expression "I am That," there is no question of anyone identifying herself with "That." It just is not possible: We can identify only with something we know. In fact, "That" denotes what remains when all that we know has been transcended. Someone who has eliminated everything in choiceless awareness will understand or feel that she is the Emptiness, the Nothingness. Then she can truly say "I am That." It may be clear now that That cannot be known, because it is not an entity or concept; therefore, it is not possible for the mind to understand it as a subject understands an object. One can only *be* That; in fact, nothing but That exists. So, after correcting our mistaken identity, we see ourselves as the Totality, as That only. Thus, through the negation of what we are not, we confirm our real identity. Realize this thing only, stabilize in this understanding, and henceforth live from that realization in all your thinking and actions.

> Hope this may have been of some help,
> Yours sincerely, R.P.

❉ ❉ ❉

Dear Dr. Powell,

I just came from a workshop with Jean Klein. I see how I "thrive" on reaction and stimulation. So who am I without the mind?

If I were blessed, I would not chatter. I am curious. I am only now beginning to inquire, it seems. Most of the time recently I am in a state of despair, in which "nothing really matters."

How can I trust the unknown? Would it help to put Jesus' name on it and become a believer? That possibility generates much emotion.

I don't expect an easy answer. Maybe I'm at a loss to ask the right question.

Do you sit in silence? Thank you for listening.

Sincerely, G.

Dear Mrs. G.,

Your problem, as described in your letter, is not really the basic problem. Fear of death is experienced by virtually all living beings, in humans to the greatest extent because of their more sensitive central nervous system and developed cognitive faculties. What is it that experiences this terrible fear and tries to overcome it? It is obviously the mind. Now, the mind can be your best friend or your worst enemy. Let me put it bluntly: it is not possible to overcome the fear of death—and it is a total waste of time to try—so long as you have not found out *who it is that dies.*

There is really only one way toward this freedom from the specter of death, and that is through *vichara,* the inquiry into the entity that has all these ideas and fears on the one hand, and That which is not affected by anything and is purity in itSelf on the other. Heed Jesus' words, to seek within, if one would find the Kingdom of Happiness. Mere belief will not do; it will not get you anywhere, but will only increase the mechanicalness and insensitivity of the mind. To cling to a belief is to sell out to some easy conceptualization; it is to live in imagination, not reality. Do not desire external things; leave off all desires save the desire for freedom, and fulfill that desire only.

The moment that we fall into a deep sleep, are we bothered by anything? Where are the desires that we restlessly pursue in the waking state, or, perhaps better stated, that pursue us? The thinking machine, which ever produces *samsara,* temporarily ceases. On waking one states: "I feel totally refreshed because I slept blissfully." While the sleeping and dying mechanisms are two different processes, they have this in common: the mind is temporarily out of the picture, and this is enough for the Self to shine in all its glory. Time and space no longer shackle us, and we are in a timeless state, the state of No-Mind, experienced as *ananda.*

Is it not clear from this that our very thinking activity is the cause—the *only* cause—of our unhappiness? The mind itself is no good in this search: since it is itself involved, it will not just lie down and die, nor will it foster any clarity in the matter. No manipulation by spiritual exercises will lead man to freedom; there is only one way, and that is to keep quiet, if only for a short moment. Then the mind becomes your best friend, the Still Mind, which no longer desires anything because it is totally fulfilled.

Do I sit in silence? Yes, and no. My ideal state is not that of *samadhi.* I lead a very active life. The mind that is alive is moving all the time, since mind is movement. It fully applies itself and meets the demands of the moment, but all of that happens spontaneously, automatically as it were. When the mind is your friend, you can leave it to do its stuff, but the Still Mind is ever present as well, in the background. It is just as with a fast spinning wheel, its rim rotating at great speed but the center point of the axis remaining motionless. So long as we do not identify with the moving mind, we never lose touch with that still center (which everybody refers to as "mySelf") no matter what activity is taking place.

Should you want to pursue this more fully, I have dealt with the question of death and other aspects of *advaita* in more detail in my book, *Path without Form.* Please let me know some time how you are faring in your search,

Sincerely, R.P.

# # #

Dear Mr. Powell,

My question is very likely the result of over-intellectualizing, inasmuch as I am a retired (but recovering) lawyer. Yet I do like clarity. I have an edition of *I Am That* brought out by The Acorn Press, with a Foreword by one Douwe Tiemersma, of Rotterdam.

On page *ix* of the Foreword, referring to the concept of "I am," he states: ". . . time and causation do not apply in reality. I am prior to the world, body and mind. I am the sphere in which they appear and disappear. I am the source of them all. . . ."

Four lines further, in the next paragraph, he says: "The sense of 'I-am-ness' is not absolutely beyond time. Being the essence of the five elements, it, in a way, depends upon the world. It arises from the body. . . ."

All I see here is contradiction. Am I missing something?

I am 74 years of age and have been turning over rocks on my "spiritual quest" since about 1953. Nisargadatta sort of blew me away. I think there is something in it for me, but I wish I had skipped that Foreword!

Best regards, R.

Dear R.,

The difference in meaning between the two paragraphs you quoted from Prof. Tiemersma is indeed very subtle, yet highly important, indeed crucial, to understanding *advaita*. The first paragraph is quite accurate in conveying the essence of the matter, which is the ultimate nature of Self, put into words, as far as humanly possible.

In the second paragraph, the key words are "the sense of, the taste of. . . ." These try to convey what we ever experience of the Self, at least in the waking state, through the medium of the five senses. It is the differentiation between the two meanings that is most essential: after all, the sweet taste of honey is not the honey. And to get this taste of the real, a sensor (that is, a body) is needed. But again, the body is not the real! It, too, is not what it appears to be, and functions only pragmatically as an aid towards an understanding of our existence. Here lie two powerful traps for students of *advaita!* The Self itself, the Absolute, is a Void in the sense of being absolutely inscrutable by any means; upon it, the world is projected as if by magic (the magic of *Maya*).

For the rest, I agree with you that terminology in treatises on *advaita* can in places become quite muddled and confusing. That is why in my Nisargadatta trilogy I prefaced each volume with an identical set of two pages of Editorial Notes on this subject. For further clarification, I refer you to these Notes.

With best wishes, Robert

⊕ ⊕ ⊕

A Word of Criticism from a Friend and a Factual Reply

Dear Robert,

If I may be quite honest as a friend of yours, the following situation has bugged me for a long time and leads me to ask this question: How can you say anything worthwhile in the spiritual area, given that you never had a proper guru yourself, but only a fleeting acquaintance with different masters? Doesn't this point to a certain "spiritual laziness"?

Sincerely, L.

Dear L.,

It is quite true, as you state, that throughout my life I have been "guru-less," for the simple reason that I have never felt the need for a guru in the outer world. I have always found it more of a challenge, more liberating, and more fun to find out things through my own capacity. By asking the right questions, we invariably arrive at a complete answer. There is nothing that we wish to know that we cannot discover for ourselves, within ourselves. All of this is, of course, only another way of describing the process of listening to our own inner guru, who is ever-present and is the very Self. In any case, this is the ultimate step for all of us, even those who have an external guru to start with. For the latter can serve only as a pointer or catalyst toward contacting the inner guru, and coming to Self-discovery.

Also true is your statement about my "spiritual laziness." Again, I find no reason to engage in the converse, "spiritual busy-ness" or even "business," because for me the spiritual life is the everyday life. No special activity or effort is therefore required. For what is there to achieve? Nor is there any "one" who could achieve. It may well be that in the beginning, to come to a full understanding of this truth, some effort, or rather "focusing of the attention," is necessary. But once you have seen deeply into your self-nature, that is the end of it and no further effort is needed. Any effort subsequent to acquiring this understanding would be like "gilding the lily," or "pushing the river." Beyond this point, you are simply "awake," and live spontaneously, with only the need to forever remain watchful.

Masters, teachings, and books are all right so far as they go, being endlessly varied approaches toward a deeper understanding of life. In their totality, they represent man's never-ending journey of exploration into the multi-faceted aspects of the body-mind entity, which enfolds the entire Cosmos. But in and of themselves, these approaches cannot lead us to reality or liberation; only our own realization can do that. They have some usefulness in the beginning when effort is still needed, but their sphere of activity is the dualistic consciousness, the "I am" state, which we must transcend before there can be unconditional freedom. And, in this connection, we must always be watchful that any *sadhanas* we might indulge in do not bring with them their own shackles. This is particularly so if a "purpose" or "goal" is attached to the *sadhana,* as is so often the case; this practice inevitably perpetuates conflict.

I am fully aware that all sorts of images of R.P. are floating around. But what can we do about them? Nothing, of course. Why should we? And does it really matter? The main thing is not to give these images any importance, and thereby avoid any identification with them. Image-making needs the presence of "others," and is the creation of "others"; therefore, it is their problem, not mine, if they wish to make it a problem.

As for myself, I simply live the ordinary everyday life and am totally content in that, needing nothing beyond it. Being "spiritually lazy," I can give full attention to whatever presents itself and needs my attention. In this way, I carry out my worldly activities not without "thinking," but without a "thinker" with all his aspirations, worldly or "spiritual." Thus, R.P. is happily stabilized in that state where we are beyond the need to claim our freedom, or defend our unfreedom.

With best wishes, Robert

❦ ❦ ❦

Dear Dr. Powell,

My name is A.F., I live in Austria, and my psychosomatic apparatus is 20 years old.

Nowhere have I found such power, authority and clarity as in *I Am That* by Nisargadatta Maharaj. Since reading it, I try to obey and follow his advice. Please Mr. Powell, can you write me some wise words on how to put Maharaj's teachings into practice?

A.F.

Dear Mr. F.,

Have you read the teachings of Sri Ramana Maharshi, especially the book, *Talks with Sri Ramana Maharshi*? I highly recommend this work for your study, in addition to Maharaj's. There also you will find strong pointers toward putting the teachings of Non-Duality into practice.

After such wonderful texts by these two great masters, what could I possibly add for your edification? I would suggest you read and re-read the above-mentioned works until you fully understand them, at least intellectually. By itself, such understanding is nothing, but without having it first as a solid backing, you cannot very well proceed beyond the intellect. Once you have such basic understanding, the moment will come that you will have had your fill of mere reading. You will then see that living the teachings is quite another matter and infinitely harder. That is when you put aside the books, for they can become a hindrance, and an excuse for staying on the level of the mind and so for procrastination.

Always bear in mind that whatever you observe, desire, fear, etc., is really the product of the mind's eye and does not really exist as such. It exists only as thought, as concept, and is within your self, not without. These are all the mind's projections, and so essentially there is nothing to desire, fear, etc., for the Self is ever fulfilled and all-encompassing. How can it be threatened, when all is Itself? But if one does not know the Self (which is man's basic Ignorance), one will ever be taken in and pushed around by thought, for obviously the mind will continue to project desires, fears, etc., *ad infinitum.* So there will be an unending series of things to desire, fear, etc., thus keeping the turmoil and mental suffering alive. A testimony to the fact that this need not be so is the deep-sleep state, when none of this wasteful and pernicious activity is going on: there is only Bliss, because in this state the mind is quiescent.

By contemplating these basic facts of our existence, we may come to understand the process of Ignorance *(avidya).* We then wake up to the falsity of our separateness or "individuality," and to the truth that there is only Consciousness, which is our Self. We perceive how the mind has created the "inner" and the "outer" through identification with the body. To put the teaching into practice is to never let any desires, fears, etc., pass from our attention without seeing how they originate from the false schism of the "me" and the "not-me."

In the beginning you will find that the psychosomatic machinery is very refractory. It is best "controlled" by leaving it alone. By taking it seriously, you assign absolute reality to it. Even to state "my psychosomatic machinery . . ." implies identification and constitutes the beginning of bondage.

With best wishes for your fruitful *sadhana,*

Yours sincerely, R.P.

✤ ✤ ✤

Dear Robert,

Thank you for your response confirming that I have articulated the matter of the "I am" closely enough. But I remain confused on its implications. I have long thought that the "Ultimate" was the concept of "I am," as often mentioned in the Bible. And in my reading of Nisargadatta's *I Am That* (admittedly, perhaps not closely enough), I got the impression that indeed the "I am" realization was the goal, which one at least moved toward by considering all that one is not. What remained was the end of one's search. And I viewed the following (typical of the biblical quotes) as saying much the same thing. But now it appears that there is something even beyond the "I am"?

Isaiah 45:6 King James Version: "That they may know from the rising of the sun, and from the west, that there is none beside me. I am the Lord, and there is none else."

Revelations 1:8 KJV: "I am Alpha and Omega, the beginning and the ending, saith the Lord, which is, and which was, and which is to come, the Almighty."

I don't propose to bug you on all this *ad infinitum,* but this one point seems basic to the teachings, and I would like to be clear on this as much as possible.

Thanks, Ralph

Dear Ralph,

I think that for intelligently discussing and possibly conveying something as difficult as Self-realization (not as concept but as actuality), the disjointed medium of e-mail messages is probably the worst imaginable. And in a way the same, but to a lesser extent, applies to books and other forms of the written word. Optimally, this is to be done through direct, face-to-face transmission, with all barriers down.

Let me just say, in addition, that the comparative approach, through the study of scriptures, etc., is usually the most confusing, and very often gets us nowhere. First, there must be some kind of discovery by and through our own inward seeking, preferably with the help of a teacher; and only then can we proceed safely toward confirmation by study of various scriptures and religious explanations (that is, if this is still important to the seeker, which it usually isn't anymore). Finally, as I wrote to you before, there is a world of difference between concept and reality, between the idea or thought of "I am," and its actuality—that is, being it. You see, the mind cannot grasp the reality of Self; in fact, it cannot even imagine it. Every concept, every thought, is a projection within the Self or Consciousness, but that Consciousness itself cannot be further defined because every thing is a mere ripple in that ocean of Consciousness. But when there is total negation, in deep Silence, of everything that the mind comes up with, then what is left is the pure Consciousness or Self.

The closest comparison to this Happiness are the bliss of dreamless sleep and the interval between two consecutive thoughts, in which only Nothingness prevails. Yet that "Nothingness" contains everything. To express this differently, one never sees a Self or "reaches" it, because if such were the case, it would only be mind stuff. And what is "reached" may be just as easily lost again. It is "experienced" (if you like that expression) as total blankness and total Silence—the absence of all fear and desire—when the mind recognizes its own futility and irrelevance in such efforts. Through It, however, everything is observed and experienced! But words can never touch the Inexpressible.

One final thing: You say you like clarity, which implies a good logical mind. This helps immeasurably, for it is only a logical mind, preferably a trained mind, that can fully apprehend the alogical (not to be confused with the illogical). Such a clear mind will know where logic applies and where it does not. When the Self is the totality, the Consciousness that underlies everything else, how can logic apply? Surely, logic can be applied only in the presence of two or more entities— in other words, in duality. Thus, the All-embracing Self may manifest a mind or a multitude of minds, but in Itself cannot appear as an experience by or in the mind (just as Love transcends the mind and cannot be analyzed or understood by the intellect). There simply isn't anything else, as beautifully stated in your Biblical quotations (e.g., "I am the Lord, and there is none else." Isaiah 45:6 King James Version).

Hope I have clarified some things.

With best wishes, Robert

⁂ ⁂ ⁂

Dear Robert:

Here I sit in front of the device that is revolutionizing communications for the world. Now the question is, do I or does anyone else have anything worth saying? Wow, what a question. . . . Let me begin by considering the use of logic in the discussion of spiritual realization. We all try to convey our thoughts in a logical or reasonable fashion. Of course, we think these thoughts within the framework of language, structured in complete sentences. Every statement and logical assertion has a subject, verb and object, and therefore contains myriads of assumptions about the nature of what is real. For example, "I am going home" assumes the existence of a separate "I" as well as a physical reality called "home." Further, there is the implied existence of space, and the concept of "going" indicates movement through that space and, therefore, time. Obviously, even the simplest of statements about our experience contains radical beliefs about our reality that have not been demonstrated to be true. So, to construct a logical argument about the nature or source of existence is to tacitly accept all of these assumptions associated with thinking and language. Of course, these are the assumptions we wish to verify, and the process presents a paradox. Our arguments depend on the truth of assumptions that our conclusion negates, such as the assumption that there is no separate "I."

It is much like the man of silence, who after years of not speaking is asked to say a few words about the virtue of silence. If he speaks, he negates the silence he extols. When we think, we deny that no-mind state of silent stillness, which is what we are.

The real question then is, can we use logic, which is thinking or mind or ego, to communicate insights that in turn invalidate the very reality of the egoity that proposes these insights? This sounds much like what Ramana Maharshi is talking about when he states: "The first thought is the "I" thought." Without the idea of a separate thinker or "I," there can be no subsequent thoughts. Is it sensible then to deny the "I" by asserting the "I" through so-called logical discourses and argument? Should we not first probe the question: "Is logic logical, and/or is it always applicable?" There may be something wrong here, and the more we think about it, the more complicated it becomes. I am in fact using a logical argument right now to discount the use of logic! A long time ago I realized in a flash of insight that the mind, with all its powers and knowledge, really did not know anything. Maybe instead of that being the beginning of a journey to discovering the real truth, it was the end.

Sincerely, B.

Dear B.,

All our musings are possible only through consciousness. Without it, there is nothing, but even the idea of nothingness can arise only in consciousness. Since consciousness is before anything, even nothingness is dependent on consciousness and is a pure concept within it.

There is no world without an observer observing that world. There is no object without a subject designating that object. Does the observer exist in your dreamless sleep? No, the world is absent because there is no one to observe it. And in your dream, the world is different from the world in the waking state, but both worlds need a dreamer to manifest. The "observer" is the "observed"! That's why to reach the Ultimate, reason alone is not sufficient—only intuition will do.

Logic is a great and necessary tool, but it can truly mislead us when misapplied to the realm beyond the subject-object relationship, beyond thought. Logic is a particular way of thinking, a special language as it were. It applies to the world of multiplicity (duality) only; it is concerned with the relation-ships of objects with one another, and with a subject. Since consciousness is non-dual, logic cannot touch it. In fact, con-sciousness is the only thing that really exists, although it is not a "thing." All "things" are only reflections within that con-sciousness. You may devise various concepts of conscious-ness and then apply logic to them, but your conclusion will not appertain to the non-dual consciousness.

The fact is that consciousness transcends logic; it reaches beyond both subject and object, observer and observed. In contrast to logic, which rules relationships, consciousness is the Self, which is the totality (non-dual). Since it carries everything within its bosom, where is the question of rela-tionship? How can it be subordinated to logic?

Sincerely, Robert

Part Three: Essays

Free Will or Predestination?

*T*he typical intellectual, especially in the West, expects clear-cut answers to the great philosophical questions of all time. But the really fundamental issues in life cannot be meaningfully viewed in terms of black and white, and perhaps not even in shades of gray. This is essentially the way of the computer, functioning rigidly within a binary system. And no computer program can reflect more than a small fragment of reality.

Man, however, has the capacity to transcend the limitations of his dualistic upbringing, which has resulted in the discursive intellect. To do this, he must go beyond all computer or computer-like language, beyond the arbitrary semantic parameters that form the atoms of his thought-world.

One of the most glaring examples of the inadequacy of the traditional approach to philosophical problems is the age-old free will/predestination controversy. If we look at this problem in terms of "either/or," there never is a solution, because any answer that comes up can always be controverted by further argument. But if we begin the enquiry by searching for meaning in our very terms of reference, we arrive at a paradoxical situation in which we see that both sides of the argument have validity, yet are not mutually exclusive. There is the ubiquitous law of cause and effect, the cornerstone of determinism; but there is also a universal intelligence that, once awakened, is free to discover the truth of causality. The seeing of causality as a fact does not rest on opinion, belief, or desire, and is therefore unconditioned; thus, the operation of this intelligence is no part of causality, although its awakening may have been.

The human mind evinces this paradox strikingly, alternating rare flashes of insight into what *is*—which are moments of absolute freedom—with long periods of cerebration (the human computer at work!), in which it is continually activated by the emotional scars of past experiences and is therefore totally in bondage. One can also make the ironical observation that man can be very creative and very inventive with regard to mechanical things, but when it comes to his own psyche he generally is highly mechanical, apathetic, and virtually completely unaware. And when the psyche is unfree, functioning like a machine, any creativity that man is capable of is essentially corrupted and to no avail in his search for happiness.

In this author's view, mankind's present psychological condition makes liberation, in the deepest sense of the word, an impossibility. No amount of yoga, "meditation" or other so-called spiritual exercises or efforts can buy us freedom, so long as our mind remains a conditioned entity whose functioning is entirely predetermined. Nevertheless, if we can bring ourselves to change fundamentally on all levels of our being, there is some hope. Such a change would spring only from a revolutionary conception of the "me," leading to the relinquishment of all aspirations for the "progress" of that "me" in the world, for it is these very aspirations that form our shackles. But we must realize that this final renunciation is a ruthless business—a kind of dying—and involves the shattering of all our "dreams," and of the various images of self that we cultivate so assiduously. Few people are ready for this, or willing to go through with it; some still think in terms of compromise, as though such a thing were possible. An unprecedented reorientation of this nature would have to go hand in hand with new thinking on other fundamental issues, such as life and death, "purpose" in the individual's life and in the Universe, and the meaning of Time—issues that are really part and parcel of the problem of the self. This new thinking will have to proceed not so much from what we already "know" (which is largely a collection of folk-lore designed to induce euphoria), but from what we do not know but have the capacity to find out through observation and introspection. In this search there is really only one obstacle, and that is our fear of the unknown. Because we cling unthinkingly to the known, which to us spells security, we block ourselves in our search for freedom—remaining in effect prisoners of our own ideologies.

On the Necessity for the Consciousness to Exist and There Being Nothing Else

*L*et us project, as a thought experiment, a reality that does not allow for the existence of a Self or Consciousness. What do we find then? Consider the approach often used in science, of making one or more approximations, as needed, before nailing down the final truth of a proposition.

It is instructive to contemplate the situation of a sleeper who wakes up from deep, dreamless sleep. At the moment of waking from his deep slumber, the world suddenly appears. That is, the sense organs at once become active, certain stirrings take place, and the "world" comes into view. The sleeper can state "I see this or that." How is it that she can utter those words?

These "stirrings" are in themselves nothing more than mechanical actions without content and without meaning—responses by the sense organs strictly on the level of physiology. We might also describe them as the interplay of computer data, minus the content or meaning assigned through human agency. Or, we can phrase this as "seeing without seer," or "hearing without hearer"—purely mechanical reactions in the total absence of sentience. In other words, there is nobody there, no conscious perceiver, and no conscious perception.

Now suppose for an instant that the Self is just a religious invention, a projection by the intellect, and not actually existing. What would be the situation then? What could be happening? The "stirrings" could take place, of course—that is, this whole physiological process involving cell physiology, nervous impulses, etc.—but there would be no Consciousness, no entity in which or by which to register them. We are reminded of the biology experiment from our school days in which an electrical current is applied to the leg muscle of a dead frog, and the muscle contracts. So it would be in a quiet, dead world where nothing registers, and no one knows or feels anything—all would simply be mechanical, physiological reaction. To all practical purposes nobody would be there, and therefore nothing would exist! This leads us to a paradoxical situation, a circular reasoning directly contradicting the assumption of an enabling mechanism on the physiological level. Nor would there be anyone or anything claiming its existence or non-existence!

Our conclusion, therefore, must be that the Consciousness does exist, must exist, to make possible everything that is as it is, including our realization as such.

FEAR OF DEATH

I have the distinct impression that the fear of death is strongly related—in fact, is caused by—the particular way we view ourselves. The following analogy may perhaps clarify the situation. It is a well-known and peculiar fact that many humans experience a fear of heights while in physical contact with the ground. Yet, they are free from this fear when there is no such connection, for example while flying in an airplane or hot-air balloon.

Similarly, the fear of death persists so long as there is any connection with a frame of reference allowing for an opposition between existence and non-existence. Such connection is a clear sign that the work of transcendence through understanding of what is, rather than what *one* is, has not yet been completed. The latter still involves separation and delimitation, because it presupposes individuation: it presupposes one who is. On the other hand, when we sever all connection with systems of knowledge, with frames of reference—all defining and conceiving of a limited "self"—we are no longer tethered to any mere ideas. We have truly left the "ground" of certainty and abandoned (false) security.

The fear of death is essentially the fear of becoming "nothing," but what if one already is "Nothing" in the first place, because one has never identified with anything? How can any fear then come into being? It cannot, because there is nothing at all, and so nothing can germinate.

When asked "Who are you?," you can say only "I don't know," or remain in silence. In truth, we are in the same position as That which appears as being dreamlessly asleep. Only in that free-floating mode, where there is no contact with a "ground" of concepts and certainty, and thereby no stake—neither psychologically nor emotionally—in anything, are we purely that which is. There is no "person" anymore, no sense of "he" or "she," or of being anything at all. The fear of death has dissolved of its own, and in fact is no longer an issue since that which carried and nourished that fear no longer exists.

FACING THE FINAL FRONTIER

*I*nevitably, to arrive at Self-knowing, at realization of the Infinite, one must first have self-knowledge; that is, knowledge of the finite, the body-mind entity that gathers this information through the five senses. And in order for sensory information to have any value, we must first know the limitations of the senses. In science this is known as determining the experimental error. Like any good scientist, we must first know the range and limitations of our tools and instruments before we can tackle the investigation.

What is the meaning of the five main senses?* And why are there just these five senses? To probe these matters, let us first do a thought experiment. What would be the situation if there were more than these five senses, say ten or more, or even an infinite number of sense organs and senses? Would a thought experiment with an infinite number of senses be legitimately permissible? I say yes, the essence of a legitimate thought experiment is that the underlying assumptions and conditions are not inherently contradictory or forbidden in any way. From an absolute standpoint, the number of senses

* To facilitate understanding of this treatment of the meaning of the senses and sense perception, it may help to read first the relevant discussion starting on page 183 of my book, *Beyond Religion.*

is arbitrary; for example, some animals have fewer or more than the five human senses available to them. (Two cases in point: bees can sense magnetic fields; penguins can see the ultraviolet range of the electromagnetic spectrum. Their perceived reality is naturally quite different from ours, and accords with the particular make-up of their senses.) The fact that there is the possibility of variability in the number and quality of senses and sense organs signifies that perception is not an absolute, and therefore that the world perceived is not an absolute. This world is relative and empirical; it is actually a function (and extension) of our physiological make-up.

If there were an infinite number of sense organs and modes of contacting the material world, then the entire concept of sense perception is moot. There would be an infinite number of worlds, and it would be meaningless to talk of perception of "the world." Accordingly, the self we think about, which we imagine we know, is ultimately empty. The real Self lies totally beyond the senses or their possible perception, and therefore beyond the ordinary consciousness. And what lies beyond—the real Self or Consciousness—cannot be projected or conceived of at all, for what is conceived in this way is a concoction of the relative plane, within the field of illusion. Since whatever lies within the field of consciousness is a product of sensory perception, thought cannot assist in conceiving of the Self. The role of the discursive intellect is totally played out. Thus, realizing that we shall never know what lies beyond the self (at least, not in the manner that we know anything else), we must fully accept our limitation. This is what I call "surrender to the Unknown." And whatever we say about It can be only in negative terms: not this, not that *(neti-neti)*. None of our ordinary experience can touch It, for It represents a total break from whatever can be conceived within and through thought. This is the final frontier: the "me" can face It but cannot cross It. We have no choice but to surrender to It.

Some readers may demur that this whole exercise in thought-experimenting, especially the possibility of there being an indefinite or even infinite number of senses, is beyond the bounds of all reason. To this, I would say only that the Self is limitless and all-powerful, and therefore nothing is impossible for It. But even on the finite level, there are intimations pointing in this direction. For example, physiologically, there is the little-known phenomenon of "synesthiology," or the joining of two senses. For example, when hearing sounds, a person simultaneously sees a certain color; that is, a fusion of two senses takes place, giving birth as it were, to a third one. And then there is the fact that under hypnosis certain individuals see pictures in color that are really (that is, consensually) black and white. Another thought-provoking phenomenon within this context is the facility that most humans possess—although few have discovered it for themselves—to physically sense the immediate boundary layer surrounding their body as a quasi-material substance with unusual texture and properties. Our fingertips can become aware of it as a sort of physical resistance. Although I am not aware that any term exists for it, I would provisionally designate it the "halo effect," and thus suggest a new kind of sensory experience.

The End of the Search

In the deepest realization there is the recognition that that which appears to exist in actuality does not, and even more significantly, that that which appears not to exist in reality does, and in fact is our deepest reality. In this way, one experiences total transcendence of life and death. Thus it is not enough to state that what appears real "is as it is," but also that that which does not appear to be real, is in fact Reality in the deepest sense.

To pursue the matter further, it is vitally important to acknowledge the impossibility of ever analyzing or understanding this latter aspect of reality. It is impossible because we are dealing with an area that lies beyond the capacity of dualistic entities to fathom, analyze, or describe. The body-mind is qualified only to describe or analyze that which lies within its sphere of operation. Ramana Maharshi once stated: "The seer sees the mind and the senses as within the Self and not apart from it." This recognition immediately limits what can be said or known about the Self or Reality, as the Totality. Thought can analyze only that which is amenable to thought, and can do nothing about the realm that is primordial or prior to thought. I am pointing more particularly to the area of reality that lies beyond the customary sphere of our consciousness: the state of dreamless sleep and the realm before birth and after physical death of the organism—the very ground state of beingness.

Because we are not aware of our fundamental limitations, we think we can treat this area of our being as amenable to dissection, analysis, and conceptualization, just as we do with everything else. We are reminded of the situation when people still thought the Earth was flat. The idea was then prevalent that by traveling sufficiently far in a straight line in any direction, one would finally reach the end of the world and inevitably fall off. Somewhat analogously, we think that the area of reality referred to above is amenable to analysis and understanding by the customary dualistic analysis, which is all that we know and can know. That which gives rise to life and so-called death, to entities and energies, to thought and concepts, is itself alien to the Totality. Not only is this Ultimate Source not amenable to dissection and analysis, but also: its range is beyond all speculation. Its very reality is the ground state for everything extant, and as such is unknowable by any means. The very mechanism of comprehension no longer applies. Its presence may be intuited but not analyzed or understood. It deserves our respect and love, for it represents our eternal, unknowable Essence, our very Self, and the area where devotion and intellect *(bhakti and jnana)* meet. Also, inevitably, it represents the end of all searching.

THE REAL IS UNKNOWABLE, THE KNOWABLE IS UNREAL

*O*ne of our great difficulties is the power of sense perception in producing various misperceptions. For what we perceive is not at all what *is*. It must be well understood that what *is* is what *is* only, and cannot be described; it can only be referred to. But we must ever be mindful of the fact that even such a reference lies entirely within the field of Ignorance, and such fundamental ignorance of our nature is a prescription for suffering.

Most people think that the basic duality lies within the apparent opposition of mind/matter, but actually therein lies no duality at all. Mind depends on matter for its existence, and matter in turn depends on mind for its perception. Each has a little of its antipode in it.

The Real cannot be perceived, for it lies beyond the field of perception, or perhaps better: prior to the field of perception. A description can be given only of entities in space and time, but the latter also are the product of sensory perception—that is, the body and its physiological processes. Perception is a function of bodily processes, and the "body" itself is ultimately a physiological, mental precept that has no ultimate reality. We are like waves in the ocean looking at other waves, but missing the Ocean in our perception.

Directly connected with this situation is the question of language and its inherent area of confusion. Existing forms of communication are based on the faulty idea that reality is tangible and communicable. Since ultimate truth is incommunicable by any means, this directly impinges on our means of communication. Thus, when a spiritual master like Sri Ramana Maharshi talks about the Self, he is not referring to any one particular individual, but to That which underlies all individuals and all observable and imaginable objects—in other words, the Totality. This Totality cannot be imagined because it lies beyond thought, and is infinitely more than an integration of finite entities.

Most spiritual efforts have as their foundation the manipulation by, and of, the mind, whereas the first requirement is the relinquishing of all efforts, all manipulation in the mental sphere. In fact, realization requires the total dismissal of the mind—for all that is based on thought and has no more reality than our imagination.

We think that we are an island in a world of plurality, where we can control or manipulate our environment to create more security for ourselves. We are totally unaware that the so-called "individual" is powerless to do anything, because there is no entity present to do anything. That "individual" is a product of the imagination. To relinquish this idea is in itself a major accomplishment because it represents a total cessation. It somehow goes against the grain of our natural state of "doing things," of making efforts to achieve results, which has become one continuous movement of incessant activity. But what we think we have moved or achieved is merely the progression of a dream and has no reality to it. Thus, all that is required is to wake up from this dream. Such an awakening necessitates the cessation of all activities and the letting go of all ambitions, even so-called spiritual goals. It means a complete ending of what one is and has always stood for. But first we must clearly see that no effort can be of any help in this, just as it is impossible to go into the deep-sleep state by making tremendous effort to "fall" asleep, as "falling" is an involuntary act. This linguistic fact points to the state of no-effort as being of the essence.

Realizing the Self as non-divisible in space and time, means there is only the "I"; all others either do not exist or are part of me, in the same way that I am part of all others. The Self is a unity in which time and space no longer have any existence. Thus, you may justifiably say with me: "When I was born, the whole Universe came into view, and with my death the whole of manifestation ceases to exist. Truly, there is only the Self and there are no others." Birth and death are verbal expressions whose referents do not exist; only the Self exists. The closest we are to this state is in dreamless sleep. To realize this in the wakeful state is to know the Ground of our being, or Self-Realization, when all differences and separations are eliminated.

This brings us finally to the question of knowledge. Since "knowledge" is always fully within the realm of thought, no amount of thought or speculation can help us in the spiritual quest. Going one step further, even the "quest" itself can be of no help to attain the Self, since such quests always deal with entities, and it is the very entities that are alien to the sphere of no-mind that is the Self. This reminds me of a discussion meeting at my house, during which one of the regular attendants opined that after many years of taking an interest in the spiritual life, his position was still that of an agnostic. He missed the point, although it is a subtle one. The agnostic, if given the magic key to understanding the universe, would only be too happy with it. His attitude is still one of clinging to one of the dualities, of not-knowing, of denying the existence of the "not-material." He does not know, but subconsciously leaves open the possibility that somewhere there exists a rational blueprint for explaining everything. Essentially, he feels the support that knowledge, even negative knowledge, gives him to carry him through life. The true *advaitin* on the other hand, who has fully seen the total irrelevance of thought and knowledge, knows that so long as the mind is involved in any way, an underlying matrix of contradiction with its special kind of pain will persist, and the Self will not reveal itself.

Finally, let us return to the question of action, especially for the purpose of realization. If all entities are unreal and of the nature of dreams, as are the actions performed with them or on them, what are we to do? This was the question asked most often during the fifteen years or so of our discussion meetings in California. Actually, it is the wrong sort of question. The simple truth is: You cannot do anything in this respect, for any such action is done by the "I," which is unreal in the first place and can therefore never lead to the real. Quite simply, when we deny the reality of the doer and recognize it as void, all action on the imagined, unreal level stops automatically and we are purely the Self. We then have awakened from the dream. In that awakening, there is no longer the "me" and others, nor the past, present, and future. All is the Now, and there is only the Now! When I was born, the whole universe and all others were born within me, and there were and are no others separate from me. And when I die, the Universe dies with me, for all are contained within me, the non-dual Self.

Seeing the light will immediately and spontaneously eliminate the darkness of the unreal self once and for all.

We wake up from the dream of unreality. But this realization excludes any sort of action, which would entail the re-emergence of the unreal. The Whole can only Be; that is, it embraces everything and everyone. It is purely the Here and Now, and recognizes no separate entities.

THOUGHT IS NOT THE ANSWER

*W*e can never escape the fact that any ultimate finding regarding our condition, any verbal definition, can never be anything but a product of thought. The greatest and most revolutionary results in science are always circumscribed by language and concept, which, however exalted they may be, are still only a product of thought, and again, expressed within thought. This is an unalterable fact. Just as the skin is our physiological border, so thought is our intellectual delimitation. The latter's expression is therefore of strictly limited value, always imprisoned by circular reasoning. This means that whether we are describing the outer reaches of the Universe or defining the nature of the self, we are spinning "mind stuff" in a self-enclosed system. Any inferences we arrive at are already contained in the original terms of our inquiry!

These very same facts underlie the general confusion as to the definition of one's self. The *advaita* literature, including statements by its most prominent sages, talks about "the Self," but by that term they do not mean the relatively narrow definition prevalent in the world of thought. Whereas in ordinary parlance "self" designates that unit circumscribed by thought and the senses, the sages refer to a Self (with a capital S), which has nothing in common with the former definition, and denotes what we are beyond the world of the senses and of thought. As such, these definitions are more useful in describing what one is not, than what one actually is. But most importantly, they may lead directly to a transcendental state beyond thought, beyond the body and the mind, where only our true identity may be found. When we cease to be occupied with the finite, with the merely conceptual, we come to lose our individuality, and realize the Self of all. By virtue of this realization, we move at once into a different dimension—the realm beyond thought, or the Silence that surpasses all silences.

The Final Barrier Is Our Very Thought

$\mathcal{M}$ost people think that knowledge is the key to everything, or almost everything, and that the reason we have not yet succeeded in realizing our Self, or Consciousness, is that we do not have the necessary knowledge. We must continue our efforts to increase our knowledge of body and mind until all ignorance has been resolved. Then, one day there will not be anything outside our ken and we shall be realized. Such an approach may be induced by either wishful thinking or self-deception, but both are simply symptoms of a fundamental Ignorance, known as *Maya*.

The fact of the matter is that realization has nothing to do with scientific knowledge of the physical world nor even with the psychological domain. This explains why realization is such a difficult undertaking: it is not an incremental process but rather a taking away of the little we know and understand of the additive process of cognition. One of the great hindrances is that what we are pointing to is not really knowledge at all but rather a state of sentience, which is prior to all knowledge and is its source. Sentience must be realized by being It.

Such a primeval state cannot be described nor taught, only pointed to. But it comes into being by itself when all ordinary channels of approach, pursued to their very ends, cease to provide further insight. Along such lines, some may say that the realized state is an empty space-time frame of reference because It represents a total Void. As phrased by Nisargadatta: "At the highest level, in reality, nothing is." But even such a primeval and "empty" space-time coordinate system cannot be brought into being and exist on its own as a separate reality; it has been projected by thought in the first place; it is still in the realm of *Maya* (illusion).

The only analogues that I can muster in this connection are the state of dreamless sleep and the short interval between two consecutive thoughts, when in terms of the ordinary consciousness, there is absolutely nothing. But even here, we might ask: What is "nothing"? How can we know it when such knowing requires a dualistic state comprised of a "knower" and a "known"? We do not really know what we call "nothing," and even more to the point: *We cannot know* "nothing"! Thus, most ordinary efforts to concretize this state are doomed to fall short of their target because they build on and depart from the ordinary state of consciousness, which is self-enclosed and thereby limited.

The realized state is totally ungraspable by the intellect and requires total surrender of all that we ordinarily hold dear. This is the first and most formidable obstacle. By its very nature, the magnitude and subtlety of the problem cannot even be adequately expressed in ordinary language, which is always the language of the mind, with its various built-in preconceptions.

Realistically, how many of us are prepared to go to the extreme lengths required of this task? Is it not a little like voluntarily accepting death—our own physical and mental demise, the death of everything we stand for and cling to? Yet, this enormous challenge is ever there, leading to the only true fulfillment. To ignore it is surely, in the deepest sense, wasting one's life.

THE ESSENCE OF RAMANA MAHARSHI

*T*he core of the teaching and the essence of what Ramana Maharshi represents in himself revolve around the question of man's identity. What we normally consider a person's identity is not his real self at all. It is derived from an ever-shifting array of superficial sensory impressions from which one has constructed a multitude of thoughts, concepts, and images, with their associated emotions. To put the matter in a nutshell, our identity is based on the apparent observation and purported existence of a particular body—the obvious product and evidence of the senses. This we take as the ultimate ground of our existence and the starting point of all thought and feeling. The body is born and dies, and in the "in-between" lies our existence, representing the precious "me." Once this has been accepted, the first person singular, and subsequently, the "you," the "we," and the "they"—the entire world of "persons" and "entities"—spring into life. And then, simultaneously, there is the Universe, which possibly has its own life and death, and so on. This is the *Weltanschauung* with which we have been brought up and which we have embraced wholeheartedly, and upon which in final analysis all philosophies and religions are based.

There is only one thing wrong with this more or less pretty picture: *the senses themselves are suspect because they, too, actually are the result of the senses.* For example, the eye that sees (although it may not be able to see itself directly) is perceived/conceived indirectly by—what else?—the eye and the mechanism of vision; in other words, the evidence is tainted—we are caught in a circular process! The seen is only evidence of a particular physiological process called "seeing." By the same token, that which we experience as "sound" has no real, independent existence as such. The impression generated by the ear-nerve-brain complex is called "sound," but it is evidence only of the particular physiological process called "hearing"; there is no "hearer" nor a "heard" in a real sense. Similarly, for other senses. Hence, the Buddha could state that "in the seen is only the seeing, in the heard only the hearing," and so on. Thus, what began as mere impressions—perhaps, quantums of subtle energy (a mode of mind indicated as *vrittis* in the Hindu literature)—is given a "body" (in both senses of the word), and becomes a focal point for all observation and activity. The entire range of our functioning is within the field of the mind—self-created, derived from this ghostlike appearance termed the "body," however deceptively it may look like solid reality. Ramana Maharshi has illustrated beautifully the origin of this continuous Self-misunderstanding as that of a policeman catching the thief who is himself!

Thus, all things and entities are *necessarily* reduced to an intangible "no-thingness," which is their ultimate Self-identity. This experiencing of the ultimate Emptiness of all relative things (their No-thingness) is at once the reaffirmation of our absolute Being—birthless and deathless (timeless), and non-locatable (spaceless). Thus, when Ramana Maharshi was dying and his devotees grieved at the prospect of the Master's imminent departure, he said: "I am not going away. Where could I go?" When this understanding is deeply and firmly sustained, we generally refer to it as "Self-Realization," where the Self (with a capital S) is indivisible and denotes our real identity. Lying beyond the field of the mind, wherein only things can be perceived and denoted, Self-Realization is not a concept, and therefore cannot be described or defined *(neti-neti)*. The Self can merely be pointed to; it cannot be described or experienced, for one *is* that Self. Only fragments within that Self can be described, but from the absolute point of view they are like footprints in the sky. What is real only is the Self, indivisible and holistic, and therefore beyond the grasp of a fragmentary, essentially unreal, mind.

Ramana Maharshi's teaching is generally associated with

that of *advaita* (or "not-two"), which runs as a vital current through all the wisdom traditions of both East and West. The term is universally used to designate this final insight into what we are and, ipso facto, the world as observed by us. It is the nature of things that anything expressed as a description or notation of reality is still itself necessarily dualistic, as otherwise nothing could be communicated. But there is one difference in this case: *Advaita* is the only concept that inexorably leads to its own destruction. Upon its full realization, it ceases to be concept! It self-destroys as concept as well as invalidating every other concept! Thus, even the very notion of non-duality becomes redundant. In sum, Reality transcends the question of *advaita* versus *dvaita*, since this formulation itself is void. We are reminded of the very apt metaphor from Buddhist teaching: the thorn needed to remove all other thorns from the flesh, after performing this vital function, is destroyed itself. Such must be seen the role and meaning of *advaita!*

In sum, Self-Realization is not a novel state to be attained; it is to realize one's present, timeless state of being through the discovery of one's true identity. The latter is sometimes described as overcoming the state of illusion *(Maya)* to which all being are subjected. But no, even this view is incorrect. As Maharshi has stated so pointedly: "the state of illusion is itself illusory." Everything is Reality and there is ever only Self-Realization, since all and everything is nothing but the Self, and one is always That only. Therefore, unbeknownst to us, we are already and ever Self-realized. It is only when we accept superficial impressions as the final word, and consequently identify with something named the "body," that we go astray and accept our reality as finite.

Consciousness Is All or Nothing as Well as All and Nothing—And So Is the Self

*F*rom a recent article by Scott La Fee in the *San Diego Union-Tribune* (March 27, 2004), we learn that neurobiologists are trying to explain consciousness. Francis Crick, the Nobel Laureate who co-discovered the structure of DNA, regards it as the major unsolved problem in biology. Its importance to this particular area of scientific investigation cannot be overrated. We should be glad that no less an eminent scientist than Crick has taken up this challenge.

More generally, I must point out a fundamental misunderstanding regarding a presumed interface between science and *advaita.* The truth is that the latter does not interface with any area of learning or knowledge, since it comprises all and everything. Even to integrate it with other concepts and attempts to define what is, lacks any kind of validity. The term appertains to the Totality, and it therefore stands outside any classification, enumeration, or designation. If we were to hint at some appropriate analogy, we could point to the realm of mathematics: Zero and infinity as mathematical symbols each standing outside any relationship to the range of ordinary, finite numbers.

Similarly, the scientific approach has full validity in its

appropriate sphere, but it cannot even begin to study consciousness or understand its fundamental nature. Science describes various processes and events that take place within consciousness, which is fundamentally different from tackling the nature of that consciousness itself. The study of consciousness raises questions about the use of investigative tools that are themselves part of the subject under investigation. A good part of the problem is caused by semantic confusion. That is, when scientists and also the general public use the term "consciousness," they simply denote the workings of the mind, or one might say "mind/body relationships." This is because it is assumed that nothing else exists or matters. Usually the term is written with a lowercase "c." *Advaitins* have introduced the capitalized "Consciousness," to differentiate it from the usual subject-object relationship. For them it signifies the totality of existence, comprising body and mind and all phenomena connected with both these terms, including the background in which they operate.

On the Superficial Level, Reality is Projected by the Sense Organs and Processed by their Extension, the Mind

The general opinion, whether voiced or unvoiced, is: "Seeing is believing." (Here one may substitute any other form of perception for the active verb "seeing.") It is a symptom of our superficial way of functioning that primarily we trust our sense organs, and all our thinking is based on that belief/acceptance. We have no desire to examine or challenge this thesis. We are like an otherwise troubled man for once soundly and blissfully asleep. Why should he wake up? It never occurs to him and would be too much of a shock, too painful altogether!

Thus, we automatically translate the superficial observation, the sensory impression, into an absolute verity. We create the entity of an "experiencer" as though there really were such a thing, while in reality there was only a momentary vision, a flash of experience . . . but by whom? We cannot say there must have been an entity to receive the impulse, because that is exactly what is yet to be proved. Always there is a stimulus appearing out of nowhere, but never any evidence of a percipient independent from the stimulus. We have taken sight as an example, but the same argument applies to the other senses.

We observe "form"—and therefore "objects"—but what do we really experience? Whatever the "object" may be, whether it be of the most "solid" nature or the most ethereal, it is experienced against a background of consciousness; without the latter, there could be no experience at all. It is just like the theatre: without a stage, there is no actor, and so no play. This is an example of visual experience, but the observation applies equally to the other senses. Ultimately all is intangible, that is, of the nature of thought or consciousness. And there is nothing more concrete or durable than that.

We may therefore view experience as a movement in consciousness. As we shift into deeper levels of being, all differentiation disappears, and all that remains as existence is consciousness. It follows that the entire range of scientific findings by Crick and other scientists is a manifestation on an entirely different level—that of dualistic or worldly experience. We must first thoroughly understand this before a new vista of understanding can open up. What we are alluding to is the question of background, or the material context of a given phenomenon, which is the domain of science. But what we are more specifically interested in is the investigation of the Background to that background, the ultimate Substrate, which is our real Essence, our real Being, commonly referred to in the literature as the Self or Consciousness (with a capital C).

Inherently, all differences are unreal, they are a question of dreaming and of not being awake. In this connection, the *Ribhu Gita* states clearly: "The concept of the world is unreal. There is nothing of form to be seen. *Sankalpa* (desire) is of the nature of unreality. The world is not the result of its activity." And in the same vein: "Existence and non-existence are only Consciousness. This disputation about 'duality' and 'non-duality' is unreal. There should be no doubt about that."

This means then that even the idea of non-duality or *advaita* is ultimately invalid and unreal, and has to be transcended, together with all other concepts! Upon full realization of this truth, there is no longer any entity; there is no more an individual entity that suffers and hopes for deliverance. Examples of such states are: the blissful condition of dreamless sleep, where the "experience" of it occurs only subsequently upon awaking; when one is connected in every possible way to a piece of beautiful music, or striking art; seeing one's life in toto without commentary on it, as in a crisis; in the intervals between two subsequent thoughts. These are only a few of the moments when we are not held by any concepts of self. Once we have had a taste of this real freedom, this limitless realm of the Self, there can be no turning back to illusory entities that defile and threaten our true integrity and peace of being.

Glossary

Advaita ("not-two"): Refers to the nature of what is, the Totality. This postulates no divisions, and so no definitions. It therefore essentially negates its entry into a glossary such as this, which must be viewed solely as pro forma. Universally used to designate the final insights into the nature of what we are, and ipso facto the world as observed by us, human beings.

It is in the nature of things that anything expressed as a description or notation of reality is still itself necessarily dualistic, as otherwise nothing could be communicated. But there is one difference in this case: *Advaita* is the only concept inexorably pointing to its own destruction. Upon its full realization it ceases to be concept. It destroys itself as concept, and invalidates every other concept as well! Thus, the very notion of non-duality becomes redundant. In sum, Reality transcends the question of *advaita* versus *dvaita,* since this formulation itself is void. We are reminded of the very apt metaphor in Buddhist teaching: the thorn that is needed to remove all other thorns from the flesh and then, after it has performed this useful function, is itself destroyed. Such must be seen the role and meaning of *advaita*.

Ananda: bliss, feeling of release

Avidya: basic ignorance, the opposite of *vidya* (knowledge)

Bhakti: devotion

Gunas: the three basic attributes or energetic/material qualities that underlie and operate the world process: *sattva* (purity, clarity, harmony), *rajas* (passion, energy, activity), and *tamas* (inertia, resistance, darkness). Everything in the material universe is said to be made of the three *gunas* in various proportions.

Jnana: knowledge, more particularly spiritual knowledge; seeing everything in absolute purity prior to the veiling of *Maya*.

Jnani: realized sage (literally: "knower")

Maya: the sphere of unreality; "the cosmic illusion, more particularly the primordial illusion of identification with the body; the manifest dynamic principle of manifestation that projects the cosmic illusion and conceals the transcendent unity."

Nama-japa: the reciting of a name of God, a technique to quiet the mind and attain constant remembrance of God

Parabrahman: the highest state, the Absolute

Prana: the vital breath, life force

Raja: energy, dynamic aspect of being

Sadhaka: spiritual aspirant

Sadhana: spiritual practice or discipline

Samadhi: an advanced stage of meditation, often described as trance-like

Samsara: empirical existence

Satori: Japanese term for the liberation experience, the transcendence of the ordinary consciousness

Satva: purity, clarity; one of the three *gunas*

Siddhis: magical powers

Vasanas: latent tendencies

About the Author

Robert Powell was born in Amsterdam, the Netherlands, in 1918. After obtaining his doctorate in chemistry from London University, he pursued a career first as an industrial chemist and later as a science writer and editor, in Britain and the United States.

Robert Powell's personal exploration of spirituality began in the 1960s, and his quest for self-discovery led him to Zen and a number of spiritual masters including J. Krishnamurti and Ramana Maharshi. His own spiritual awakening coincided with his discovery of the teachings of Nisargadatta Maharaj. He is the editor of a Nisargadatta trilogy, and the author of a number of books on what he describes as "human consciousness transformation." Powell now lives a busy life in La Jolla, California, with his loving wife, Gina.